STRANGE INTRUDERS

**Based on interviews and research
conducted by David Weatherly**

ISBN 10 - 1945950005 (Paperback)
ISBN 13 - 9781945950001

Published by:

EERIE LIGHTS

**Eerie Lights Publishing
Nevada**

Cover by: Sam Shearon
www.mister-sam.com

Editor: A. Dale Triplett
www.daletriplett.com

Interior design by: SMAK Graphics
www.smakgraphics.com

Printed in the United States of America

To John Keel:
"Not an authority on any thing," but an inspiration nonetheless.

Praise for David Weatherly's,
The Black Eyed Children

"David Weatherly's research is top-notch, and he goes where other researchers fear to tread! Thanks for bringing this phenomena into the light of day."

- L. A. Marzulli, author of *On The Trail Of The Nephilim*

✢ ✢ ✢ ✢ ✢

"Well-written, informative, and downright creepy, *The Black Eyed Children* will make you think twice about answering a knock at your door."

- Lyle Blackburn, author of *The Beast of Boggy Creek*.

✢ ✢ ✢ ✢ ✢

"*The Black Eyed Children* is a jam-packed, balanced report on a developing phenomenon now stretching across the world. The exceptional reporting of the facts is reflected in David's ability to sympathize with the eye witnesses, drawing out the story which for many has been a traumatic ordeal, and one they never wish to face again. The book is an excellent addition to everyone's book collection with an interest in all things supernatural, and will promise to leave you with haunting and intimidating questions."

- Barry Fitzgerald, author of *The Banshee* and *Searching for the Sidhe*.

✢ ✢ ✢ ✢ ✢

David, like a few other researchers, examines all of these phenomena from multiple perspectives: paranormal, crypto, ET, shamanic, cross-cultural, and others. I subscribe to that as well. We all agree that a broad approach is the only way to figure out the big picture of human involvement with other beings. *The Black-Eyed Children* will have a prominent place in my research library."

- Rosemary Ellen Guiley, author of *The Djinn Connection*.

"David Weatherly's *The Black Eyed Children* is a fascinating, insightful and remarkable piece of work on a subject that has been crying out for a definitive study - and now, we have that definitive study."

- Nick Redfern, author of *Monster Diary, The Real Men in Black* and *Wild Man*.

"Altogether, I am proud that a guy like David Weatherly is willing to risk life and limb to go looking for trouble—find it—and still manage to come back alive and tell the rest of us about it."

- Micah Hanks, author of *The UFO Singularity*.

Table of Contents

Acknowledgements

While writing sounds like an easy process, the reality is that it entails a great deal of work and the patience and assistance of those near and dear.

My work, as always, is a tribute to the love and support I receive from family, friends and colleagues. Personal support came in many different forms during the completion of this book. I'm truly blessed to have some amazing people to call friends, and I don't for a moment wish to exclude any of them, so consider this a blanket thanks to those who I haven't mentioned by name.

There are tons of pioneers in the field of exploring the weird and unexplained, and any of us writing on such topics owe them a debt. Charles Fort, John Keel, Jacques Vallee, Hans Holzer and many others placed the bar high by looking at such phenomena from numerous perspectives, always asking questions and always questioning answers. Their books have always proven valuable and inspiring, and they kept me up for many a late night.

Special thanks to artist supreme Sam Shearon for an amazing and creepy cover that captured the essence of my intent with this book. I honestly didn't know what to expect, but took a leap of faith, and the result was well beyond my expectations. I just hope the interior does justice to the artistic representation.

Thanks to my southern brother, Mr. Micah Hanks, for an introduction that was truly a pleasure to read, even if it was about my book. Anytime I'm compared with the legendary John Keel, I take it as a compliment. It's a pleasure to have a foreword from someone who thinks outside the box when it comes to strange phenomena.

Thanks to my Irish cohort in trouble-making, Barry Fitzgerald. He's always a great one for a laugh and to share a pint with. I'm proud to consider him one of my closest friends.

Thanks to Nick Redfern for ideas and laughs. Nick, your writing output continues to amaze me; I'd like some of your mojo, so please, ship a bottle out!

Thanks to Lyle Blackburn. We always seem to attract... unusual experiences when we're hanging out... which means we probably should do so more often.

Thanks to William WhiteCrow, a brother on the path of spirit. I appreciate your service to the country, and your continued service to all the people you help.

Of course, most of all, thanks to all the people who shared their accounts of weird phenomena and strange experiences with me.

- *David Weatherly*

Foreword

"This material is to be shown only to individuals who have a need to know. It should be kept in a very safe place, under lock and key at all times."

Thus were the words on the cover of the otherwise relatively plain looking folder, with a simple title appended to the top of the page: DOCUMENT 1-Q.

It was 1967, and the indefatigable journalist, world traveler, and starving author known as John Keel had been pursuing an all-new mystery in the state of West Virginia. Reports described it as being very large and winged—though at times, there would be a variety of different things described, ranging from a large bird, to a large man-like beast covered in white fur. If anything, it had become difficult to put a finger on any singular phenomenon, and even to begin in hopes of roughly categorizing this present "it" that had captured the young reporter's fascination.

The mainstream press, on the other hand, went steadily to work, and famously tagged the strange happenings in West Virginia Keel had witnessed firsthand as a UFO flap, and then later on, the literal presence of what many began calling a "Mothman."

This strange affair would become what Keel was best known for, and perhaps somewhat tragically, as it had been the events surrounding the so-called Mothman that would later, according to Fortean scholars, become associated with one of the greatest infrastructure failures in modern time: the collapse of the Silver Bridge, a large eyebar-chain suspension bridge that connected Gallipolis, Ohio with nearby Point Pleasant, West Virginia. The bridge, which failed and collapsed during rush-hour traffic on December 15, 1967, was believed by many to have been a singular event of some kind; an event that may have been foretold by omens, or some series of secretive warnings. Thus, a host of different conspiracy theories and other popular beliefs have become associated with the accident over the years. As for Keel, he claimed that he too had been in contact with different sources—some of them not entirely of this world—that had somehow alluded to this oncoming disaster before it ever occurred.

Of this semi-spectral culprit, the Mothman, and of his apparitional nonhuman ilk, Collin Bennett wrote in 2002, "These supra-human forms are quite conscious, aware, and active. In West Virginia, Keel found the local 'systemanimal' had its own agenda; it 'spoke' through simulacra and weather, atmosphere and geology, coincidence and dream. Before the coming of Christianity and science, such forms as Keel describes were a fully understood part of an integrated world image that linked mind to sacred sites, landscape, ideas and evolving culture. They were part of the knitting together of matter and idea, body and soul." For Keel, it had been very much the case that he felt certain intelligences were communicating with him through the very foundations of an "evolving culture," as Bennett puts it. Although there certainly were times the otherwise disparate language of myth, dream and symbol would strike far closer to home, sometimes erupting into overt, direct communication with alleged nonhuman entities.

This brings us back to the plain-looking dossier Keel kept for so many years, detailing alleged correspondences Keel had been having with one called "Mr. Apol," a supposed ultraterrestrial introduced to Keel by his associate, a woman named Jaye Paro. It is unclear whether Apol was in direct contact with Paro, or if they were even one and the same. "As far as I can tell," Keel's long time friend Doug Skinner wrote in early 2013, "[Paro] was channeling him. Apol's answers are interesting," Skinner notes of the series of curious exchanges Keel had shared with Apol in 1967. "But John's questions intrigue me more: these are the things that he wanted to know. He clearly valued the correspondence at the time, and believed he was getting valuable information. But, of course, these damned ultraterrestrials, whether imaginary or not, are not to be trusted…".

Keel had methodically gone about asking questions, which "Apol" would respond to, always with a red-colored pencil. "On August 4th, 1967 a large manila envelope turned up in my mail-box," Keel stated, "containing questions with the answers awkwardly written in red pencil." Keel had sent the initial "questionnaire" along through "channels that have been open to me for some time.

"Our visitors can neither read nor write," Keel explained, "but [they] can understand our writing through a complex mechanism of multiple senses. It is apparently difficult for them to hold and manipulate a pencil… They even have trouble drawing straight lines, as my previous experiences have shown me… The visitors probably spent a great deal of time and effort in filling out this questionnaire."

"DO NOT TAKE THIS DOCUMENT LIGHTLY," Keel says toward the bottom of the introductory paper contained with the questionnaire for Apol. "It contains important clues to the phenomenon and offers some vital information." As far as the actual content of that questionnaire, perhaps Skinner was correct in asserting that, in many cases, Keel's questions represent the more interesting portions of the exchange. Keel begins by asking about six military planes that disappeared off the coast of Florida in 1945, alluding to multiple ongoing disappearances of military aircraft alleged to occur in tandem with UFO sightings.

Among other questions Keel sent to Mr. Apol were such curiosities as, "Have I done exactly what you expected?" and "Are you pleased with what I have been doing?" Regarding fellow researcher Gray Barker, one of Keel's contemporaries who had been the first to write publicly about the menace known as "Men in Black," Keel had bluntly asked whether Barker was, "being controlled", and whether he "is being controlled by you (Apol)." According to the strange scribbling of Keel's otherworldly pen pal, Barker was being controlled, in fact, though not by Apol or his ultraterrestrial missionaries; instead, it was suggested rather conspicuously that Barker was under the control of Apol's "enemies," and that he had indeed been under such influence during a previous phone call in July of that year, which Keel asked about specifically.

What, if anything, can be made of these strange correspondences Keel kept for so many years? If anything, it seems obvious Keel believed at the time, and throughout various times in his life, that he had been receiving strange communications, perhaps from nonhuman beings, and from time to time they passed along information to him that no one else of this world could have known.

As a Fortean researcher myself—or perhaps, to put it more concisely for modern times, being what I prefer to call a Keelian researcher, in honor of John's strange and often deadpan journalistic style—I feel there have been inexplicable instances in my own life, where information has been imparted to me by individuals who otherwise could not have known the details they passed along, unless they had received such information by unconventional methods. On at least two occasions, David Weatherly has managed to succeed in doing this, and while I wouldn't presume he is a nonhuman entity (nor do I suspect he is under the overt control of some Keelian ultraterrestrial intelligence, as poor Gray Barker had appeared to be), I do feel part of the unique connection we share has to do with our mutual interest not only in Keel, but in the strange nonhuman presence that many would argue remains in our midst even today.

Weatherly's previous offering detailed famously the ongoing saga of the "Black Eyed Children," a phenomenon that, if there is anything redeeming to say about this otherwise terrifying mythos, is that it has far less to do with domestic abuse than the casual observer may take from it's name at a glance. Rather, the Black Eyed Children are akin, in many ways, to Barker's MIBs, and even to Keel's "weirdos" he often described meeting during UFO flaps, in that these odd-looking "children" appear on one's doorstep, saying troubling, or even disturbing things before attempting to enter the home. But the most striking aspect of the BEC encounter, as the name would entail, has to do with the fact these "children" are reported to have ghostly-looking, solid black eyes. Indeed, there is an almost emotive unsettling quality to these meetings, which lends itself to the notion evil may not only don black-colored garb for purposes of intimidation; sometimes, it seems to literally emanate from within.

While black and darkness remain preferential tastes among the bogeymen and coal-eyed miscreants of the nonhuman underworld, there are other forms these characters have been known to maintain. From the large and lurching "Grinning Man" Keel himself recounted (and whom Weatherly not only cites fascination with, but claims to have literally seen), to the leaping louts of Europe known variously as Spring-Heeled Jack, Perak the Spring-Man, and Jumping Jack Flash, our haunted little planet seems, at times, to be riddled with complaints by those who profess having seen something they cannot explain, often which involves a being or other monstrosity that simply terrified them.

So, yet again, here with the present volume, Weatherly soberly goes about his pursuit of this world's strange mysteries, matter-of-factly pinning himself against the edifice of oddity's very lodging, and expecting to uncover the truth about what mysteries may lie waiting within its darkened walls.

To wit, I say, better him than me! While I'm happy to crawl amidst the dolmens and ditches of Earth's hidden history, or even to occasionally pursue the great monster of forgotten lore to its lair, there are times where some of these nonhuman "weirdos," as Keel had affectionately called them, become simply too unsettling for one to have to deal with of his own accord.

Thus, altogether, I am proud a guy like David Weatherly is willing to risk life and limb to go looking for trouble—find it—and still manage to come back alive and tell the rest of us about it. Enjoy this book, and the approaching perusal of its pages that you are about to undertake. With little question, what you'll find here will leave you wondering, as David and I have both been forced to do more than once, whether this world we think we know might be riddled with its own unique varieties of hidden residents that peer at us constantly from the ever-present shadows of myth and imagination, as well as the fringes of our modern society and culture.

Above all, as Keel had so famously warned, do not take this document lightly! For better, or for worse, the information you'll find within its pages may one day prove useful to you, should you ever be unfortunate enough to have that unsettling experience yourself: of meeting eye-to-eye with a strange, nonhuman, Keelian entity the likes of which you thought could never really exist.

They do exist... and for all you or I know, they may be watching you right now.

- Micah A. Hanks
Somewhere in Appalachia, North Carolina
February 24, 2013

"The oldest and strongest emotion of mankind is fear, and the oldest and strongest kind of fear is fear of the unknown."

– H. P. Lovecraft

Introduction

The old man took a long drag on his hand-rolled cigarette. He held it a moment, then exhaled slowly, looking up to the sky while the smoke drifted off with the wind.

"A long time ago, there were other ones here. They lived on the earth, just like we humans do, but they were different. They had different ways. When the people began to spread out across the land, the other ones didn't like it. They decided to leave. A great hole opened in the earth, in the side of a mountain, and those other beings, they went in. Then they sealed that entrance up from the inside. They can come back whenever they want to, but we can't find the way to get into their world. We shouldn't try to find it anyway; it's a dark place."

Native cultures around the world have such legends, tales of other races, other beings, who lived and walked here on the earth, sharing the world with humankind. At some point, these other races left. Sometimes, it was due to a war with humans; other times they indicated they were going back to their own world. Often it was unknown exactly why they left. Their point of exit is variously described as a hole in the earth or a mountain, a window in the sky, or a shimmering doorway, a portal to another world, another level of existence, a bridge to their home or a lost land.

The idea of other worlds and dimensions beyond ours may seem far-fetched to some, but mainstream science has embraced the theory. As the quantum sciences move forward they merge into territory previously reserved for spiritual concepts. Ancient knowledge long taught by older cultures is suddenly being 'proven' by science. Ideas once only part of the fabric of spiritual belief systems are now being seen as quantum concepts to be refined and explored by scientists. An article in the Science Daily discussed the concept of other dimensions:

"The mathematics of string theory suggests that the world we know is not complete. In addition to our four familiar dimensions -- three-dimensional space and time -- string theory predicts the existence of six extra spatial dimensions, 'hidden' dimensions curled in tiny geometric shapes at every single point in our universe.

"Don't worry if you can't picture a 10-dimensional world. Our minds are accustomed to only three spatial dimensions and lack a frame of reference for the other six, says UW-Madison physicist Gary Shiu." (*Science Daily, Feb 4, 2007*)

Indeed, the modern mind is not accustomed to thinking in terms of multiple dimensions, but that doesn't mean they don't exist. The question we should be asking is this; just because we don't know how to get into other dimensions, does that mean beings from those other dimensions can't get here?

Again, traditional cultures already provide the answers. Ancient belief systems speak of beings able to traverse the paths between our world and the next. Some call it the otherworld, some have dubbed it the dreamtime. They all say, it is as real as our existence here. And the ones who live in these other worlds? They are spirits, fairies, even the souls of the departed. Some are beneficial, others dark and devious and all seem to have access to our world.

The Djinn, Black Eyed people, Pukwudgies, the Grinning man, Reptilians, the list of weird beings goes on and on, reading like the roll call of a science fiction series. It would all be considered a grand delusion by many people, but the list of these creatures grows, and the number of accounts does likewise. They can manifest any time of the day or night, in quiet homes, or on busy streets. What do they want? Where do they come from and why are they here? These and other nagging questions hang in the air like the trail of cigarette smoke puffed out by the old shaman. Physical, present - but elusive and impossible to grasp or fully understand.

For as long as man has lived, tales have been told of such strange beings. The stories are rich with accounts of alien beings from the sky, odd encounters with the paranormal, urban legends with grains of truth and weird criminal behaviors from humans who are obviously not so normal. The lines between all of these things are often blurred, melding together to further obscure reality into a strange unfolding of not-so-normal events.

Some of these visitors are aggressive, pursuing their victims with ferocity and anger, causing terror until their magical time is suddenly finished and they vanish from whence they came, leaving no trace. Others are in stark contrast to such violent behavior, simply appearing by the roadside, a mocking smile plastered on a distorted face. Still others hide in the shadows, masking their intent in the darkness.

They appear unbound by our natural laws, and, in fact, seem to relish breaking the natural order of things as we understand it. Some fly, some melt into the shadows, others are simply... gone. All in the blink of an eye, unclear to us and disturbing in their unknowable nature. While their intent is not clear, one thing is. They do not belong here. They are alien, intrusive and most often, sinister. Always, they leave questions in the wake of their departure, especially the most troublesome one, will they return? Whatever the case may be, they follow their own patterns and directives.

Some of the accounts you'll find here could perhaps have normal, mundane explanations as they reside on the very edge of strangeness. Others are at the opposite end of the spectrum, bizarre beyond imagining. Nonetheless, with all of them, lingering questions remain, adding to the air of mystery created by the encounters.

As John Keel wrote in *The Complete Guide to Mysterious Beings*:

"The most fearsome monsters of all may inhabit the dark corners of our minds waiting for us to release them through our beliefs and gullibility. The phenomenon feeds on fear and belief, sometimes it destroys us altogether, other times it leads us upwards into the labyrinth of electromagnetic frequencies which form a curtain in the areas we call "windows," and they stalk us to drink our blood and create all kinds of mischievous beliefs and misconceptions in our feeble little terrestrial minds."

We are experiencing a time of high strangeness and the number of weird encounters grows on a daily basis. Perhaps part of this is due to the current popularity of all things paranormal. More people than ever are now anxious to experience something strange and beyond ordinary. This is a two-edged sword as it leads to more mistakes and more jumping to conclusions than normal. On the other hand, people are more open minded and pay more attention in an effort to understand the weird. I relish seeing so many people asking questions, seeking answers and exercising their curiosity.

Contained here you will find a collection of strange beings, or 'strange intruders' as I have termed them. Here are monkey men and reptoids, shadow people, and grinning men, trouble-making pukwudgies, and oily men. And there's more, much, much more. Some are likely weird criminals, some perhaps animals, and others... well, they remain unknown and perhaps they are visitors from...

somewhere. My goal is to report the events and to give you the accounts that remain bothersome on some primal level.

If I've done my job properly, then you'll find some answers but a lot more questions, and really, that's what this field is all about. Asking questions and continuing the search for the truth behind these strange tales. However, a note of caution if you think you know the truth. Step back and ask yourself that question again... for the answer could be much stranger than you ever realized.

Chapter One
The Mysterious Djinn

From the Mysterious Desert

The deserts of the Middle East are strange, forbidding landscapes, a dramatic contrast to the bustling cities and green forests to which much of the world is accustomed. Romantic images from the *Arabian Nights* and the exploits of Lawrence of Arabia may spring to mind, but these are mere distortions, westernized versions of the stark reality of the desert. Here life is a precious thing, vulnerable to the elements, the scarcity of water, and perhaps, to supernatural beings that live just beyond our perception of reality. Natives who are frequent travelers of this mystic landscape stay on guard, cautious of such beings who are usually unseen to the human eye. In these ancient lands, such spirits are known as the djinn.

"It is on long journeys across the sands when the risk of encountering the djinn is highest," Nazim told me.

"It is because when you travel far, you will cross the territory of many different djinn, and you must have their permission in order to pass. Otherwise, they will harass you, or worse, possess you."

Nazim is from the Middle East. A long time Sufi and mystic, he is well versed in the lore of the djinn and their influence in the world. He is frequently called on to assist those plagued by the troublesome entities. Nazim had early encounters with the legendary djinn. While growing up and spending time in the desert, he had many strange experiences that he believes could only be explained as being djinn.

"Sometimes in the desert, you will hear music; it comes from nowhere because there is nothing as far as you can see. This music is the djinn. They are invisible to us unless they want to reveal themselves. I have been in the deserts and heard their music; it is an eerie sound. Also, they will throw stones at you sometimes. Again, there will be nothing as far as you can see, no other people.

Three of us were out together one night, it is safer in groups, but we were not safe that night. The djinn pelted us with stones, small ones about the size of a quarter at first, then larger ones. We got away as quickly as we could, saying prayers the whole time."

Some believe if you ask permission of the djinn, they will let you pass through their territory, but it is wise to never depend on such things. The djinn are not to be trusted, it seems, and are notorious for bending agreements or breaking pacts. Sudden gusts of wind, sandstorms that rise up as if from nowhere and even shooting stars are reputed to be signs that djinn are in the vicinity. Sometimes a pillar of sand will rise up and within it may be seen the form of a djinn. There are also tales of travelers seeing phantom camps or villages appearing as if a mirage in the sands. These are dangerous places and it is possible to be caught in the land of the djinn if one dares to step into their boundaries.

Nazim has lived in the United States, the UK and several different Middle Eastern countries. He reports that the djinn have spread far beyond the borders of the countries they are most commonly associated with, and believes that his upbringing in the Middle East, combined with his education in Western countries, has given him a unique perspective on the djinn.

"In the worst cases, a djinn can take possession of someone. In lesser cases, they can take up residence in a home or place of business where they will cause trouble. Some people believe that the djinn are merely tricksters, and while it is true they like to play pranks, their agenda is much more serious and sinister. Left alone their simple pranks will escalate. They will quickly go from stealing or misplacing objects to starting fires or causing accidents."

Aside from the Middle East, I have helped people plagued by the djinn in America, England, Scotland and other countries. These beings do not recognize nor care about borders or countries. They will go where they please and can travel quickly and with great ease. While people in many Eastern countries know about and respect the power of the djinn, in the Western world they are more of a joke and people do not take them seriously. This only seems to anger the djinn and create openings for them to take even more advantage.

If a person gains the attention of a djinn, then the spirit will not let go, it will follow that person and harass them until it achieves its goal. The goal of such djinn is often to drive the person to madness, or perhaps to cause death. I have worked with many, many soldiers who attracted the notice of a djinn while they were stationed in the Middle East. When they go back to their home country, the djinn will follow them. I am saddened to think of how many soldiers are plagued by such things yet do not know what the true source of their trouble is."

The Western world knows them better as "genies," a term that conjures up comical images of fat, blue men in curly-tipped shoes and baggy pants granting wishes, or perhaps a goofy blonde living in a bottle. The reality of the djinn is far, far from this perception. According to Islamic lore the djinn were created by Allah, one of his three sentient creations, the others being humans who were created from earth and angels who were made of light. The djinn were made from "smokeless flame" or "scorching fire" and they were expected to worship Allah and follow the teachings of the prophet. But in the early days of creation, Iblis, the head of the djinn rebelled. In front of Allah, Iblis refused the order to bow down to the authority of Adam, believing humans were inferior to djinn. For his actions, Allah cast Iblis and his followers out of paradise and banished them to the wild deserts. This origin story is one of the reasons djinn are so often equated with the desert.

Djinn are said to live in a world parallel to our own. They can be good, evil or neutral. They are known as "The Hidden Ones" and do not exist in the way humans do. They can live in the sand, in the ashes of a fire, even in the wind. They do have a society and traditions, however, they can lead individual lives with families and relationships. They may even follow a particular religion or spiritual path. Those that are positive beings are less likely to interact with the human world at all.

Some tales say the Djinn live in vast cities that lie beneath the sand of the deserts. Others believe they are everywhere, inhabiting places such as graveyards, wastelands, caves, and deserted buildings and cities. In the Middle East, it is common to avoid such places rather than risk encountering these entities. Scholars believe the number of djinn is vast and that while they do have cities on their plane of existence, they can also inhabit our world. Uncontrolled and unrestricted, the djinn seem to be able to live wherever they please.

There is some evidence the djinn were worshiped in some regions. This, however, is believed to be a dangerous path some equate with the worship of demons. The Quran specifically warns against the worship of djinn:

"Yet they make the jinn equals with Allah, though Allah did create the jinn; and they falsely, having no knowledge, attribute to Him sons and daughters. Praise and glory be to Him! (for He is) above what they attribute to Him!" Quran 6:100.

The lore of the djinn attributes a diverse range of powers to them. They are able to travel vast distances in the wink of an eye, live to be thousands of years old and are not restricted by time or space. They possess knowledge far beyond that of humans. They can shape-shift into virtually any form, human, animal, tree or even inanimate objects. They can take possession of living creatures and control both the mind and body of their victims. They can take the form of deceased loved ones, and appear to the living in ghostly form, or within dreams. These powers and more are part of the arsenal of djinn abilities, and it is why they are considered such a serious threat in much of the world.

Encounters with the Djinn

Traditional lore says that speaking about the djinn too much, or too loudly, will attract their attention and cause them to trouble you. They often take their time, lurking about and learning as much as they can about a person to decide how best to take advantage.

According to Nazim:

"Like a spider, a djinn will very slowly spin a web until it surrounds you. He will tell you what you wish to hear and appear as a helpful spirit. He will even tell you to pray and follow spiritual teachings. He will do whatever is necessary to draw you in until you are trapped. Once you go willingly, it is very difficult to get away. The djinn can drive you insane."

One of their favorite tactics in fact, is to slowly torment an individual's mind, leading them on the path to insanity. They can appear as vile creatures in the physical world, only letting their intended victim witness them. They can create nightmares and constantly disrupt sleep. At times they will pretend to be helpful spirits, professing their desire to assist and guide. They can whisper to their victim, imparting information others could not possibly know, leading to the appearance of prophecy and psychic ability. While such

4

information may be beneficial at the onset, the agenda is inevitably dark, and the djinn will slowly lead their victim astray.

Such a sinister unfolding of djinn influence is evident in a case Nazim had involving a service man who had been involved in the Iraqi conflict. As Nazim recounts:

"In 2009, I was called on to help a man who was living in the UK. He was a former soldier and had spent time in Iraq before and after the fall of Saddam Hussein. When he got out of the service, he went to live with his new wife in a home in the UK; he wanted to forget about the Middle East. Things were not good for him. At first, he got a job with a friend from the service but he had many problems and lost his job. He got another, but still had problems. He could not sleep because he would have constant nightmares, causing him to wake in a cold sweat. He became a very nervous person; he would be overtaken with a shaking, nervous motion in his arm. Doctors could find nothing wrong with him and later it got even worse, the shaking spread to both arms. He had difficulty driving sometimes, difficulty eating even. Then it got worse yet again. He started hearing voices when he was awake. At first, it was just a few times a week, but they began to become more and more frequent. He would hear them at home, at work, everywhere. He started believing that he was hearing his mother who had died years before. The voices would tell him things that no one else could have known. But the number of different voices increased. He was put on medication, but it only made things much worse, so on his own, he came off the pills and consulted a religious person. In fact, he tried several different religious people. Some of them helped to a degree because he found that after blessings or religious attention, he would be a little better for maybe a few days. One of the people he went to told him to look to the east because his trouble had started there. The suggestion was that he suffered a mental illness from his time there but it gave the man another idea. He went to a spiritual person he knew who was Muslim. This man told the soldier that his problem was most likely a djinn. This is the short version of how the man came to me for help. When I spoke with him, right away I felt that djinn were involved because of the things he was suffering. I did some things to help him rest more. His health improved a little with the blessings. By our third meeting, I had him start telling me about his time in Iraq. I wanted to know about the things he had encountered, the things he had seen and experienced and, most important, I wanted to know if he had brought anything back. At first, he said no, not really. "Just personal items and a few things I bought in a market." He showed me these items and nothing

5

was suspicious. I continued to help him, cleansing the home, seeking answers, giving protective amulets to him and his family. Sometimes, one must be patient and wait for the djinn to reveal itself or for the answer to come another way. It was on our fifth meeting that things became clear. When I walked in, he was excited and said he had to show me something. He brought out a small piece of cloth and sat it on the table.

"I had forgotten about this," he said. "I found it in some rubble when we were clearing an area outside of a city. For some reason, I couldn't resist picking it up and keeping it. I stowed it in a small pocket and forgot about it, but when you asked if I had brought anything back, it kind of nagged at me and I knew there was something I couldn't remember. My mind has been so foggy though, that I could not think what it was. Last night though, I felt a little better and decided to go through all of my things again. That's when I remembered a small pocket and something I had tucked away."

I carefully opened the cloth and inside was a small ring. It was not too fancy, there were three little stones set in it and the metal was worn, it looked old. I would not say it was of particular value, at least not in terms of money. I knew right away that this was the source of the man's problems. I told him that the ring was connected to the djinn that was tormenting him. With his permission, I took the ring away and dealt with it. His health recovered, the voices stopped and he began to lead a happy life."

Nazim's account is one of a djinn clearly connected to a specific object. We will never know exactly why or how such a connection occurred, but the important thing is that the man's life and health was given back to him before it was too late.

A similar case came to me in 2007 when I was approached by Brandon, a former US soldier who believed his family's home was being haunted by a poltergeist. After investigation, there was little evidence to support the presence of a poltergeist and the activity in fact seemed to center around Brandon. Knowing about his time in the Middle East, I began to question him about his experiences there to determine if "something" had returned with him to the states.

One very interesting incident came up:

"We were ordered into an area that was in really rough shape, not just from the recent conflict, but from a long time before. The locals kept saying that we shouldn't enter this one particular building but of course, we had to check it out to see if anyone was hiding in there. It was a creepy place. It was obvious that it had been empty a long time and it didn't even appear that anyone had been in there in forever. The thing is, there was this weird moment when I could have sworn someone was standing right beside me, like they were inches away staring in my face from the left side. I've never believed in the supernatural, I always thought it was all crap, but after that experience, I never quite felt the same. I got out of the service as soon as I could and I came home. Not long after that, this ghost activity started at our house."

After learning more details, it turns out Brandon had entered a building reputed to be a dwelling place of the djinn. Was his strange encounter a djinn attaching to him? After going through a process to rid him of djinn influence, the activity in Brandon's house stopped and life returned to normal.

It would seem from such cases that soldiers are especially vulnerable to the djinn. Western military operations in the Middle East have indeed presented the djinn with a range of new victims to which they can attach.

While the stories of these soldiers are of chance encounters with the unknown, there are cases where people intentionally connect with the djinn. In a discussion with Nazim, he told me he had seen numerous cases of this occurring.

"I have had people come to me who willingly made a contract with djinn, and these are some of the most disturbing cases. I always consider if only they had known what they were dealing with. But at the time, they believed the djinn had good intent and was a helpful spirit. Of course, it will not identify itself as a djinn. In all my experience with these beings, I do not believe that there are any such djinn out there; I believe that they are all of evil. In every case I have had, it always comes back around to the djinn having an evil intent and of working only towards its own desires. They are very smart, very deceptive and they are patient. They will wait a long time before their true purpose is revealed and along the way, they will drive a person to madness."

It is in fact rather easy to summon the djinn because they are always waiting for such opportunities to freely access the human world. Whether it is to take up residence in someone's home, or to take up residence in someone's body, they are ever ready and eager. But the djinn cannot really be confined or controlled for very long. As tricksters, they are adept at setting traps for those who try to contain their power. They can detect an individual's weakness or vulnerability and will use it to their advantage without a second thought.

The Djinn in Love and War

The djinn have a strong presence in Southeast Asia where they are part of many aspects of culture. Muslim practice has blended with native traditions, creating a unique set of ideas and spiritual beliefs. Ideas about the djinn can be rather complex in this part of the world. A wide range of types of djinn are present. As in other countries, djinn will readily take up residence in abandoned buildings and homes. Curiously, djinn are also to be found around Mosques. Some are seeking redemption by listening to holy teachings, others are there in an attempt to lure humans away from spiritual practice.

Silat is a generic term for indigenous martial arts from Southeast Asia. There are hundreds of different forms of the art throughout the region, and many of them contain aspects considered magical. This can mean working with various forms of energy for healing or combat, magical potions made from herbs and other ingredients, or working with and binding spirits such as the djinn. Originating in Indonesia, the arts have spread to Vietnam, Malaysia, the Philippines, Thailand and Singapore. While not all versions of Silat are practiced by Muslims, many of them are and they integrate their beliefs related to the djinn.

A Silat teacher from Malaysia who I worked with told me that djinn are often to be found even within the martial traditions of his country.

"Some masters of the art will utilize djinn to increase their own power. I knew a teacher who wore a ring on the middle finger of each of his hands. He claimed that he could use them to summon powerful djinn. They would give him an advantage in combat. They could cause his opponent to be struck down with weakness or illness. This is a dangerous tactic, since it all depends on his continuing ability to control the spirits."

Another Silat teacher of my acquaintance from Jakarta told me his sister was "cursed with a djinn" when the family moved away from Jakarta.

"There was a young man who was fascinated by my sister and had designs to marry her. She was not interested in him, she wanted to go to school and get a degree. And marriage —especially to him— was not in her plan. Within a week after our family moved, she became ill. She started to sleep long, long hours and we had much trouble getting her out of bed. She was taken to a doctor and they said that it was probably a flu and they gave her some pills, but these did nothing for her. She began to look very pale and she would not eat much. Finally, our mother called upon a holy person. He said prayers over her and she reacted very strangely. He asked for her bags from the move; some of them had never been unpacked. He started going through them asking her about different items. Finally, he found a small metal box. He asked her about it, but she had never seen it before. "But it is in your things," he said. He opened the box and I don't know what he saw inside, but he closed it quickly. "You have been cursed with a djinn" he told her. I must take this away and deal with it. After this, my sister recovered quickly. She believes that the man who was in love with her slipped the box into her bags when he came to see her off—An act of revenge from a rejected man."

According to Nazim, a lot of the people who come to him for help against the djinn have fallen into trouble because of lust.

"I have had many, many cases of those who made a contract with the djinn attempting to gain the object of their desire. They mistakenly believe that the djinn will compel someone to lust after them and return their affections. Sometimes this works at first, but it is always a trap. If the djinn put two people together, it will often turn the relationship into a very dark, destructive one because it was built on a false foundation. You cannot use magic or beings like djinn to force someone to love you though some people are so driven by their desires that they cannot resist what seems to be a powerful way to get what they want. I always tell people that the djinn cannot bear to be around the true power of love since it overwhelms their evil intent."

Houses of the Djinn

Due to the djinn's attraction to abandoned buildings, some sites develop a strong association with their presence. One of the most notable is the legendary city of Petra.

The ancient city of Petra is one of the most famous historical sites in the Middle East. The most popular tourist attraction in the small country of Jordan, Petra was named a UNESCO world heritage site in 1985. Its stunning rock-cut architecture has led to its use in numerous films such as "Indiana Jones and the Last Crusade" where the site was portrayed as the final resting spot of the Holy Grail, the legendary cup of Christ.

Petra, which means 'stone' is known as the "Rose City" because of the coloring of its rocks, the stunning rock-carved city is quite wondrous to behold. Arab tradition says the city is the spot where Moses struck a rock with his staff causing water to come forth. The site is also the burial location of Aaron, brother of Moses. In ancient times, a mountaintop shrine to Miriam, sister of Moses, was located at Petra, but the exact spot has been lost to the ages.

Beyond the history and spiritual connections, there's another side to Petra. It is plagued by the djinn. Locals say the ancient city is a very dangerous place to go, especially in the late hours of the day or at night. There are reports of rocks being thrown from out of nowhere, a common djinn tactic. The loud clashing of metal echoes out of various chambers deep within Petra, the sound of sword fighting, or so the locals believe.

Visitors who dare to stay at the location in the latter half of the day have reported ghostly apparitions, strange sounds and whispers, and shadowy forms moving among the rocks. Those who believe in the djinn say the figures come out in an attempt to possess unwary visitors at the site. Numerous people have reported hearing their name whispered from inside the building, an attempt by "something" to pull them deep inside the mysterious chambers. Some even believe the whispers to be those of deceased relatives calling to them from beyond.

Even security guards who work at the site are cautious and fearful, taking every measure possible to protect themselves from the sinister djinn.

There are many such sites to be found in the Middle East. In the UAE (United Arab Emirates) there is the deserted village of Jazirat Al Hamra, ancestral home of the Zaabi tribe. It now lies empty, fallen prey to the elements of the encroaching desert around it. The village is filled with old-style adobe homes, abandoned mosques, and djinn. While some dare to roam around this abandoned place, most locals avoid it for fear of encountering djinn that have taken up residence and claimed it as their own.

Saudi Arabia has a valley known as "Wadi Al-Amak" or "the deep abyss," a dreaded place believed to be haunted by nasty djinn, responsible for a number of possessions, even in recent years.

Places such as these and others are a vital part of the traditions in this region of the world. Here, the djinn are simply a reality, something that must be considered and guarded against. Popular in this region is the blue talisman, a ward against the evil eye and protection against the djinn. While some may consider it superstition, it is deeply rooted in the belief systems of the region, and for the people living there, the talisman seems to work.

But the djinn are not restricted to cities in the Middle East; their influence can be found all around the world. Parts of the Mediterranean, Central and Southeast Asia have all seen outbreaks of djinn activity. The troublesome spirits are also well known on the east coast of Africa.

Nigeria has been a hotbed of djinn activity for many years. Here, tales of the djinn have blended with legends of the "iskoki," African spirits long known to the country's natives. Modern Nigeria has seen the djinn exert an influence, even to the highest levels of government.

In 2002, Abdullahi Dan Gusau, close ally of the Zamfara state governor was arrested on fraud charges. His defense — he was forced to commit crimes by an evil djinn. Gusau was accused of forging the governor's signature on a document in order to defraud certain individuals, a crime to which he admitted guilt. According to Kaduna's newspaper, the *"Weekly Trust"* of September 6:

"He (Gusau) claimed that he was compelled to act by some supernatural forces. According to him, by the djinns. The case is before the court for adjudication."

There is a large population of Muslims in northern Nigeria, and like many other places, people there are cautious around abandoned homes and buildings because of the supposed presence of djinn.

Kenya has suffered outbreaks of djinn activity in recent years. Nairobi newspaper *"The Standard"* printed an article in its June 30, 2008 edition titled "Evil Exploits of the Invisible People" by Caroline Mango. In the report she detailed attacks in Mombasa that were being attributed to the djinn. Area residents claimed they were being beaten, slapped, strangled and even sexually assaulted by invisible attackers.

11

Many of the encounters and sightings were centered on a number of vacant houses in the old quarter of the city. Although the homes were beautiful, those living in them reported troubling activity that forced them to abandon the houses. Apparently these nice homes had become uninhabitable by humans because aggressive djinn had moved in.

An old town resident named Mohammed went on record about some of his experiences: "One moment you see naked people and the next they are dressed. At other times, you hear invisible people talking and laughing around you."

Indeed, around the abandoned homes, area residents reported hearing "invisible families" talking and moving about inside the empty buildings.

Additionally, strange people were spotted wandering around the streets at night, there one moment and gone the next.

Another cluster of strange activity seemed to be focused around nearby bridges, including a number of sexual assaults occurring to both men and women.

Secretary General of the Supreme Council of Kenyan Muslims, Sheikh Juma Ngao, was quoted in the article. When asked about djinn he replied that the djinn were real and live like normal human beings. Asked about their presence in Mombasa, the Sheikh replied; "Some like living in the sea, others prefer the hills, while some stay in exile in forests and deserts. Some might actually be living on top of your roof, that is just their preference."

India too, has its share of djinn. The Muslims and Hindus both tell tales of the beings and some work with the djinn seeking to use their magical abilities for beneficial reasons. Some Sufis in India believe the djinn are not all harmful and attempt to cultivate relationships with them.

William Dalrymple, who has written an excellent book on Delhi titled *"City of Djinns,"* met a Sufi who informed him about the magical beings. While in Delhi, Dalrymple spoke with the Sufi, named Pir Sadr-ud-Din at great length. The Sufi had spent forty-one days half-naked and without food in the foothills of the Himalayas, and then later, another forty-one days up to his neck in the river Jumna. The Sufi prayed throughout this process, all of which was part of the path to gain the ability to see the djinn. Pir told Dalrymple that the King of the Djinns later appeared to him while he was asleep in a graveyard. According to Pir:

"He was black, as tall as a tree, and he had one eye in the center of his forehead. The djinn offered me anything I wanted, but every time I refused."

The city of Delhi, according to Sadr-ud-Din, is a city of djinns. The Sufi told Dalrymple that the djinn loved Delhi and lived in every corner of it, in every house, building and on the streets. Since they are invisible, most people are not aware of them. According to the Sufi:

"You could not see them...but if you concentrated you would be able to feel them: to hear their whisperings, or even, if you were lucky, to sense their warm breath on your face."

The presence of so many djinn is the secret of Delhi's long existence. The Sufi believe the djinn will never let Delhi fall, nor will they let it become deserted or abandoned. The djinn, he claims, will always help Delhi rise from destruction and be reborn.

Corking the Bottle

Legends of those who try to control the djinn go back to biblical times. The earliest tales relate to the biblical King Solomon who captured the sinister djinn and used them for labor. The process of capturing the djinn was one of ritual and magical technique sorcerers throughout the ages have sought to recover. Solomon enslaved the djinn and forced them to build and work in his temple. According to the Quran, Solomon bound the magical beings and made them perform tasks while he was king. His control of them was so great, in fact, they continued to serve him even after his death. We find details of this in the Quran:

"And before Solomon were marshaled his hosts, of djinn and men and birds and they were all kept in order and ranks" Quran 27:17.

The Quran says Solomon died standing upright while leaning on his staff. The djinn, unaware the king had died, continued to perform their tasks lest they face the mighty king's wrath. This continued until Allah sent a worm out of the ground to eat away at Solomon's staff, causing the king's body to collapse. Again, we find details in the Quran:

13

"Then, when we decreed (Solomon's) death, nothing showed them his death except a little worm of the earth, which kept gnawing away at his staff so when he fell down, the djinn saw plainly that if they had known the unseen, they would not have tarried in the humiliating penalty." Quran 34:14.

Legend says that once free from the king's control, the djinn became even more vengeful and angry. Since they had suffered such a long period of captivity, they set out on a quest to manipulate and control humans whenever possible as revenge for their humiliation.

During his time, Solomon captured and imprisoned other djinn, sometimes in bottles or flasks, sometimes within stone columns. It is believed some of the stone pillars in his famous temple held mighty djinn.

Medieval magicians, fascinated with early biblical tales, believed it was possible to recreate the feat King Solomon had accomplished and trap djinn for their own use. If a force as powerful as a djinn could be contained and made to do the bidding of the jailer, untold possibilities were suddenly open.

Some legends claim certain sorcerers, magicians and Sheikhs (Islamic holy men) were actually able to accomplish this. By all accounts, it was a path fraught with danger and risk. A djinn who was summoned but not bound was likely to take its anger out on the magician attempting to trap it. Furthermore, due to their deceitful nature, any dealings with djinn were dangerous and it was just as likely the sorcerer himself would end up as the one trapped. Despite the risk, magicians have continued to attempt this through the ages. In Delhi, author William Dalrymple asked for the secret to capturing djinn. He was told:

"It is a great secret. The art was first discovered by Solomon and passed on to the dervishes of his time, long before the age of the Prophet Muhammad. Even today, the great dervishes still keep this secret. They cannot pass it on to anyone but another master dervish."

Magical texts from the past, known as grimoires, detail the ceremonies and rituals designed to summon and entrap the djinn. Who hasn't heard of Aladdin and his wondrous lamp, complete with a djinn inside? Such tales, along with Solomon's ability to trap djinn in objects, have laid much of the foundation for the modern interpretation of genies in lamps.

Using ancient grimoires, and trying to mimic Solomon, magical practitioners would call forth djinn and bind them to physical objects; often, it was a piece of jewelry such as a ring, necklace or bracelet. This made it possible for the magician to carry the djinn's power with them wherever they went, calling up the entity at will in order to force it to cast the evil eye, cause illness or other malicious tasks. Magicians who chose to conceal any symbol of the djinn would bind it to a larger object such as a bottle, lamp or mirror. This item could be kept in the magician's workspace and accessed when needed.

Defending Against the Djinn

Over the years, numerous tactics have been developed to defend against the djinn. I have listed some of the most prominent here. Bear in mind, these techniques may seem primitive to many westerners, ringing of superstition and folk magic. In truth however, these methods have been used for thousands of years and to cultures native to the region, the methods work as well as the practice of Christians sprinkling holy water. As with many such measures, the true power may simply lie in the belief in the process.

It should also be noted that traditionally, Muslims believe any protection from supernatural beings must come directly from Allah. Traditional Muslims believe reciting the final three chapters of the Quran (112-114), is the greatest means of protection against all evil forces and creatures including, but not limited to, the djinn. As a result, the practice of wearing talismans, amulets or using and employing magical means to deal with djinn is not approved. But as with all things, there are exceptions to the rule. Amulets are allowed in Islam under certain conditions. First, they must contain the names of Allah and his attributes. They must also be written in Arabic. Furthermore, those who employ such amulets must realize the words in the charm only have effect because Allah has empowered them.

Many tribal communities still adhere to traditional and ancient magical remedies. Remote areas of the Middle East are rich in such lore and it is from these traditions we find the old ways of dealing with the djinn. These sources have no qualms about mixing ancient techniques with modern Muslim beliefs.

Salt is considered a good, primary defense against the djinn since they hate it. It can be used in food, carried in the pocket or put in shoes and even under a pillow at night. Some sprinkle it around entryways, windows or on the floor. Throwing salt in the air is advised if there is a need to walk around at night, one of the most dangerous times to encounter djinn.

Iron, steel and silver are also considered valid defenses against the djinn. Some people wear metal rings on their fingers or on necklaces. A nail worn on string around the neck is popular in some areas. Knives kept under a pillow will ward off djinn as will coins added to bath water.

Loud sounds also seem to be a deterrent. The clash of cymbals or the sounding of horns or other instruments are often used to clear an area of the troublesome djinn. A Greek-American associate of mine tells me that he and his friends keep firecrackers handy for use in areas suspected to be the hiding places of djinn.

Christians who have encountered the djinn have reported success with using the Lord's Prayer as a defense. Others have called upon Saint Michael the archangel with his fiery sword, a resource often called on to defend against evil forces by Catholics and Protestants alike. Christian symbols and holy water have also proven to be effective in some cases. Again, much of the power is in the belief or faith within the person wielding the item.

By far the most popular protection against the djinn is the wearing of an amulet or talisman. As noted above, Muslims may wear or hang an amulet made to specifications that adhere to their religious beliefs. The most common of these amulets is the "ta'wiz" or tawiz. The tawiz is a small, black, cloth pouch usually worn around the neck. It contains a small paper inscribed with prayers written in Arabic. The paper is folded a specific number of times before being closed in the pouch. Such talismans are especially popular among Muslims in Pakistan and India.

Another type of amulet that is used extensively around the world is known as a "nazar". This is an eye-shaped amulet usually made of handmade glass. It features concentric circles in white, blues and black. Sometimes the outer edge is ringed with gold or yellow. There are many uses for the nazar. Although it is commonly worn as a pendant, it also features in other types of jewelry. Rings, bracelets, anklets, even earrings can feature a nazar. The beads come in many sizes and are often sewn into clothing as a protective measure. Artistic versions of the nazar are popular since they can be hung in homes to ward off evil. It is common to find them hung in places of business, near the cribs of newborns, even in vehicles. While the nazar is most often prescribed as a protection against the evil eye, it is also utilized as a defense against the djinn.

A Growing Presence

In November 2012, BBC News released a documentary by reporter Catrin Nye titled "Possession, Jinn and Britain's Backstreet Exorcists."

This documentary took a serious look at the growing number of people in the UK promoting themselves as healers able to cure people of djinn affliction. While the report focused on the concerns of UK health and social workers and their attitude of disbelief towards the supernatural, it was significant in that it addressed the djinn. In the now racially diverse UK, large communities of Muslims from different countries have taken up residence bringing their customs and beliefs, including their belief in the djinn, with them. This has led to a support system of practitioners who also believe in the evil spirits and who make their living exorcising those who become afflicted. One practitioner interviewed by Nye, a Mr. Mohammed, primarily uses the Quran for his healing work. He states:

"I cure them by this book (the Quran). You have to have faith in it and it will work. So yes, anxiety, depression, heart problems, many, believe me, many problems get cured by this healing."

Paranormal investigator and author Rosemary Ellen Guiley has done a vast amount of work researching the Djinn, and her books on the topic are an excellent resource that I highly recommend. According to Guiley, the Djinn may actually account for a large portion of encounters with various paranormal entities attributed to the likes of demons and even extraterrestrials. While the existence of other such beings is still a possibility, the shape shifting Djinn may simply be using cultural concepts of such things in order to influence humans.

Are the djinn really this powerful? And if so, why has there not been more attention focused on these strange entities? If Guiley is right, then we hardly understand the scope of the djinn's true power. In the west, the djinn are still relatively unknown players in the world of the paranormal. While some may think these beings are new on the scene they are actually an ancient presence we are still trying to understand. If these beings are even half as powerful as research indicates, then the implications of a widespread djinn presence is a

17

potential matter of great concern. Scholars of the past were aware of the potential problems the djinn could cause, and much of their work, filed away as mythological studies, may offer insights into what we are truly dealing with.

In a classic essay on the djinn, Islamic theologian Ibn Taymeeyah (1263-1328) says:

"No one in any of the Muslim sects denies the existence of jinn or that Allah sent Muhammad to them."

He goes on to state his belief that the power of the djinn account for much of what passes for magic. Mimicking the voices of the departed during seances, revealing hidden secrets to fortune tellers and assisting magicians are all djinn tricks he believes are designed to deceive humans. Taymeeyah says that the djinn are generally:

"...ignorant, untruthful, oppressive and treacherous."

If the djinn truly have the ability to shape shift, then it would be easy for them to insert themselves into the lives of people unaware of the existence of such beings. In the United States, few people have any sense that the djinn are a valid concern, and even in the Middle East, home of the djinn legends, many modern scholars dismiss the whole thing as myth.

Robert Lebling, author of *"Legends of the Fire Spirits,"* an in-depth study on the djinn, addresses this:

"Many in the West are unwilling to concede the existence of jinn (which is their Arabic name). This reluctance is grounded partly in a rationalist tradition, which rejects the existence of most things that cannot be seen or experienced otherwise"

"It may come as a surprise to many in the West to learn that jinn are taken seriously and regarded as real, tangible beings by a large segment of the world's population. Millions of people in North Africa, the Middle East and other Islamic regions have been brought up to consider jinn as a normal, natural part of the world around them."

Cases of paranormal phenomena show that ignorance of the phenomenon does not necessarily make one safe from it. Closing our minds to the possibility of the djinn will not cause the cases to go away.

As Rosemary Ellen Guiley states in her book, *"The Djinn*

Connection":

"The Djinn are real, and we need to know about them, and how they are affecting our world and our pursuit of our own destiny."

Indeed, it seems the presence of the djinn is growing, and for the most part, we know very little about what we may be dealing with, or what the potential of the djinn's abilities truly are. That ignorance may prove to be a dangerous thing.

Chapter Two
From the Shadows

A Deepening Shadow

Shadow People. Over the last few years, they have become one of the hottest topics in the world of the paranormal. While reports of these beings go far back in history, encounters with them began reaching a peak in the early 2000s. Radio programs like Coast to Coast AM became popular outlets for those who wanted to share their encounters with these creepy beings.

Shadow people cause high levels of fear and terror in their victims. As the name implies, they are humanoid forms that appear to be made of pure darkness. Victims commonly state the beings are 'blacker than black,' a darkness deeper than the unlit rooms they appear in. These menacing black forms are most often reported appearing in bedrooms, lurking in corners, emerging from closets or looming over people who are sleeping.

Some victims report attacks by these shadowy beings. Crushing pressure applied when the shadow form pushes down on them making it difficult to breathe. There are reports of physical sensations as the form strikes out with dark limbs, at times, leaving marks that are discovered later. Others report the shadow beings attempt to drag them from their beds, intending to pull them off to some dark netherworld.

Shadow people cross the spectrum into many corners of the paranormal. They are often found in homes but have been known to appear outside, from open fields to cemeteries. They are experienced by people of all ages, men and women alike. They have been blamed for poltergeist-like activity, and physical attacks such as scratches, slaps and bruises. They create general disturbances in homes, pushing items off shelves and making loud noises. They can cause important things like keys and jewelry to go missing. Many victims say the shadow people project anger and hostile energy and that they are responsible for invoking nightmares. They seem to come and go at will, emerging from mirrors or dark spaces. Sometimes they manifest out of thin air. Like the classical boogeyman, they can appear from under beds or slide out from under closet doors. Some victims report a strange black smoke that appears with the shadow people when they appear or depart.

At times, they are vague, shapeless forms, barely human in shape. Other reports claim they appear as tall men wearing hats and long coats. Older reports link them to phantom monks, dark figures wearing robes with large hoods over their heads. Only rarely are physical features seen with the exception of glowing red eyes. Their movements are reported as being quick and jerky, often the shadows move suddenly from one location in the room to another. Some people claim to see them disappear into mirrors, solid walls, floors and ceilings. On occasion, they will convey messages. Sometimes this is done telepathically but there are accounts of heavy, raspy voices issuing statements from these dark forms. Usually, the messages are as menacing as the beings themselves.

Often, the victims find themselves frozen in place, unable to move as the shadowy form creeps about the room, moving to their bedside and leaning down as if to examine them. This inability to move has led some scientists to claim shadow beings are nothing more than a form of sleep paralysis, and the entire experience of shadow people is in the mind. While this broad proclamation may account for a portion of the accounts, it certainly cannot explain them all. Often, these encounters take place when the victim is fully awake and conscious. On these occasions, victims experience other elements of the shadow beings. Physical contact has been made, predictions have been given and the sense of being in the presence of a very real being is much more prominent. "The shadow people radiate pure evil and malicious intent," one victim stated. Indeed, from most reports, the negative energy emitting from shadow people is so strong many victims are convinced the beings are demons attempting to manifest fully onto the earth plane. This belief is prominent within those of the Christian faith who have had encounters with the shadow beings.

The Gospel of John

John is a good example of this mindset. This John is not one of the twelve Apostles, but still a man of faith. He firmly believes shadow people are pure evil and connected to some demonic force, the devil if you will. He further believes they appeared in his life at a time when his faith was at a low point and the trials of dealing with them put him back on a spiritual path.

John says his personal experiences with shadow beings resulted from his lack of attention to his spiritual life. He reports he started encountering the shadow people once he stopped attending church on a regular basis. At first, the manifestations were brief, fleeting glimpses of shadowy forms seen from the corner of his eye. Over the course of several months, the sightings began to increase along with his sense of a presence within his home. He tried to brush it off and ignore it but the shadows only became more active. He started seeing them in his direct field of vision and they would boldly move across the room while he was eating or watching television. Still, he tried to ignore the incidents, passing them off as stress or exhaustion from long hours at work. It became harder to deny that something was wrong when the physical manifestations began.

"I would be sitting at my table and I would see a quick movement, suddenly a utensil would go flying off the table or something would fall off a shelf to the floor. One day it was a bag of flour that just exploded while it was sitting on the kitchen counter. Another day, a dish flew out of the sink and smashed on the floor. I saw a shadowy form standing in the corner by the sink. I could have sworn that I heard something laughing. I was getting worried, but all I did was throw myself more into my work, figuring that it would all just pass, that whatever it was would stop if I was able to ignore it."

John dealt with the shadow people in his home for a little over a year. His encounters escalated from simple, quick sightings of the dark forms to direct views of the beings. But soon things took another turn for the worse. It was late September when John had a dramatic encounter that included a very frightening, physical attack:

"I had worked late and then grabbed a bite to eat with a friend at a local burger joint. I got home about 9:30. By the time I looked over the mail and checked my email it was a bit after 10:00, and I decided to head to bed. I went into my bedroom and sat down on my bed. I didn't turn the light on because the streetlights from outside gave the room some illumination. I kicked my shoes off and sat on the side of the bed a moment. I was just looking out of the window at the trees when all of a sudden I felt something grab my ankles. It felt just like

23

hands, one on each ankle. Before I could even think, I was yanked really hard and fell forward to the floor. I was on my stomach now and whatever it was, it was pulling me hard, trying to get me under the bed. I turned on my side and moved a little, reaching out to grab hold of the radiator that was against the wall. Thank God it was mounted firmly into the floor. I managed to get my other hand up and I was now holding the radiator with both hands. I looked down towards the bed and from what little light there was, I saw what looked like a man-sized figure under the bed, pulling at me. The two arms were projecting out from under the bed. But the most disturbing thing was that I saw two glowing red eyes looking out at me from under the bed. I started trying to pull my legs back, kicking them around and yelling at the thing to get off of me and to leave me alone. I felt desperate. I felt like, if this thing was able to pull me under the bed I would be gone. I don't know what I thought would happen or where exactly I would go, I just believed that I wouldn't be here anymore.

I was always a fairly religious person. I grew up going to church and had gone most of my adult life. I had taken a new job that was very demanding and I simply hadn't had much time to devote to the church. Now, in the face of this attack, I started to pray. I was calling the Lord's name and saying every prayer I could think of. I don't know how long I struggled with it. I'm sure it wasn't as long as it felt like it was. Eventually, I felt like the thing started to weaken, then I hear what sounded like a growl coming from it. It only encouraged me to pray louder, pouring everything I could into it. I truly felt it was my only defense against the creature. I was still kicking my legs and I suddenly felt one of them break free. I pulled it up and placing my foot on the floor, lurched forward towards my nightstand. I had to let go of the radiator to do it but now I held onto the nightstand with one hand and with the other yanked open the drawer and pulled out my Bible. I held it up towards the creature and continued to pray. Just as suddenly as the attack had started, it stopped. It was over and the thing was gone. I got up quickly and turned on all the lights. I kicked the side of my bed, I still thought the thing was under there and I wanted to see it in the light. I was daring it to come out and I was still praying. Finally, I pushed the bed aside, expecting something to be there but there was nothing."

While those of a non-religious nature would think John was having a delusional episode, he firmly believes he experienced a physical battle with something demonic. Did his personal faith and trust in a higher spiritual power really save him from a dark end? On a personal level, John doesn't care whether others believe his story or not.

"I know what I experienced and I know some people won't believe my story, but that's not my concern. I've talked to lots of other folks who have encountered these shadow people. The things are dangerous and for those like me who experience the terror of having these things in your home, it is frightening. I pray with people all the time now who are facing these creatures and the darkness they bring."

Other victims who have had violent, physical encounters with shadow people are left with the psychological trauma of the experience, and the lingering fear the beings will return to attack again. In some cases, the shadow beings suddenly end their visits and never harass the victim again. Other times, the shadows return, continuing to torment their victim on a constant basis.

Overall, John's encounters with the shadow people lasted for a fairly short period. Many of those who deal with shadow beings report being plagued by them for years, and in some cases, throughout their entire lives.

Laurie is one such victim. She began experiencing the shadow beings when she was a very young girl. The first incident of significance occurred when she was only twelve:

"I've seen shadow people since I was a child. It started when I was very young, but the incident I remember the best from the early part of my life happened when I was about twelve years old. My younger sister and I had bedrooms that were right across from each other. If we left our doors open, we could easily see into each other's rooms. My father had bought new dressers for us both. The dressers had big mirrors on the tops. Mine was put on my far wall, but my sister put hers on the wall across from her door. This meant that if our doors were open, I could look into her room and see her dresser and the mirror. I didn't like that mirror being there like that. Our parents made us leave our doors open at night. If I got up to go to the bathroom, there would be strange reflections in the mirror in my sister's room. I told myself that it was just from car lights passing by or that it was from my own reflection, but it still bothered me. For awhile, I just wouldn't get up unless I really, really had to.

A few weeks probably went by and one night, I had to get up in the middle of the night to go to the bathroom. There was a little lamp that always stayed on in my sister's bedroom and it cast a lot of light around the front of the room where her dresser was. When I was walking out of my room, I noticed a large shadow moving across that part of her room. I thought it looked odd because it was so tall, I knew shadows would do that, but it had such a weird shape. I stopped in the hall right between our rooms and looked at it. The shadow stopped moving and I thought, oh, it's my shadow moving like that. I stood there for a minute and I could have sworn that I heard breathing as if someone was standing there. I thought it was just my imagination and I turned to go down the hall to the bathroom. When I started to move, I noticed that the shadow did not! I froze. I turned and looked directly at the shadow, then I started to move my arms around to see if the arms of the shadow moved, they didn't. All of a sudden, I felt very afraid. I moved backwards towards my room, and when I reached the doorway, the shadow suddenly moved, it was now in the hallway outside my sister's door. I thought it was coming towards me and I screamed. It was pretty loud and after a second, I saw a light come on downstairs. The shadow had been still, now it suddenly darted back into my sister's room. It hit the mirror over her dresser and it was gone. In a moment, my mother was upstairs asking me what was wrong. I tried to tell her all that had happened; she just shook her head and said that I was only dreaming. I insisted that it was not a dream, but she just sent me back to bed."

Laurie reports that her encounters with shadow people continued throughout her life. Regardless of where she lived, the shadow beings would turn up. Fortunately, Laurie has never suffered direct attacks from the beings. That's not to say that she has not been deeply affected by her experiences. The psychological effect of something always lurking in the shadows has left her disturbed and at times, feeling very unbalanced. Often, the shadow beings have glowing red or yellow eyes, and she reports that sounds come from them at times.

"I don't even feel like I've lived a completely normal life. Wherever I've gone, the things show up. It's not that they physically hurt me, but the sense of something watching like that, it's terrible because I don't feel like they're positive or protective. I've had breaks from it, but in some ways that doesn't even help because I spend time wondering how long before they return. I've tried a lot of different things from people who tried to help get rid of them but they always come back. I've had months without them; then all of a sudden one night, there they are coming out of the hallway or just suddenly appearing in my room in a mist of black energy."

Conjuring the Darkness

What causes these beings to manifest and why do they haunt some people for such long periods? Data is still being collected, but there are some patterns to which we can pay attention.

Shadow people seem to appear often in connection with traumatic, emotional events. Locations where murders or tragic deaths have taken place are common areas for the shadow people to manifest. One theory is they either feed off the emotional energy, or are created by it as an aftereffect. As with poltergeist cases, teenagers are often a catalyst for the shadow beings. Again, this may be due to a biological/energetic effect. Raging hormones and the struggle to understand emotions along with the search for identity are powerful components for any mixture.

One of the most interesting correlations found in the appearance of shadow people is their connection to the occult. It seems dabbling in the occult or magical practices has been known to instigate encounters with shadow people. In these cases, the activity often increases at a rapid pace and the results are often long-term. Combining an interest in the occult with the trials of teenage life makes for an especially potent combination — case in point, Rebecca.

When she was a teenager, Rebecca moved with her parents to an older home in eastern North Carolina. It was a fairly normal town and the family had lived in the area for awhile, so Rebecca didn't lose her connection to her friends or school. The house was a foreclosure her father purchased at a bargain price and needed a lot of work. But it was big and it meant Rebecca and her siblings would all have their own rooms. In short order, Rebecca made a startling discovery in the home.

"I got to pick my bedroom and I took the one that was upstairs, at the front of the house. It had a big walk-in closet that had obviously been part of the main room originally. The whole house was a bit odd really. It was old and people had tried to upgrade it piecemeal, a lot of things just didn't fit right. In my room, someone had built a wall to create the closet and it had sort of a weird angle.

It was only a couple of weeks after we had moved into the house that my best friend, Rachel, was over hanging out. I was still in the same school because we had only moved across town. We were lying on the floor talking about people at school and I was kind of staring around the room. I said something to Rachel about the closet and that it was weird how it had been built. Rachel replied, that yes, it was weird and that she thought my room would be bigger because it was a pretty big house. It got me thinking about the fact that my room did seem small. I got up and leaned out the window of my room, just looking at the house. I was thinking that yes, my room should be bigger.

Rachel and I went in the closet and I was pushing against the wall of it because it seemed flimsy. I was actually afraid that it would fall down and into my room. I had put the bed on the other side of the room because of this. When I pushed against the wall though, I heard another sound from the back corner of the closet. Pushing against the main wall made some boards on the other wall move. We went to the corner and I could see that the boards were very loose and it looked like light was coming through those boards. I pulled one away some and I could tell there was another room behind it. Now I knew why my room was smaller, there was another space boarded up behind the closet wall.

Rachel and I were both excited and we pulled away at a couple more of the boards and removed enough of them so we could crawl through. We went into the little room. It was pretty dusty in there. There was a small window up high; from the outside, I had thought it was an attic window. There wasn't much in the room except an old wooden chair. Around the floor there was a lot of wax, you could tell that someone had burned a lot of candles in there. Rachel was staring at the floor and said that she thought something was drawn on the wood floorboards. We used our shoes to scrape away some of the dirt on the floor. What we found was a big pentagram drawn in the middle of the room. We figured someone who used to live there had been doing witchcraft in the room."

Like many teenage girls, Rebecca and her friend Rachel were fascinated by the idea of practicing magical arts. The girls were teenagers in the mid-nineties when 'Wicca' was experiencing a phase of popularity and countless books were being published on the topic. The idea of being 'witches' had a certain allure of mystery, and hinted at powers others didn't have. Rebecca did not report the hidden room to her parents, instead, she and Rachel, along with a third friend formed a 'coven' and began practicing rituals they found in books on witchcraft. Rebecca took the discovery of the hidden room as a sign they should be practicing Wicca. Their practice became a mishmash of various belief systems, mostly in an attempt to gain psychic powers and the ability to influence other people to do their will. They also attempted to tell each other's fortunes with tarot cards and other fortune telling tools. On some level, Rebecca claims, they were just 'having fun' while on another level, they were genuinely hoping to gain some kind of insight. Their rituals became more elaborate, they played with a Ouija board, recited spells they had found in books and even tried making a voodoo doll when a high school boy angered the three of them, with what they considered an affront to their coven.

It was no doubt the formula for countless B-grade horror movies, but it was the reality of the belief system the girls were developing.

"I think, at some point, we really started to identify ourselves as witches. It became all we talked about and all we wanted to do. Our parents ignored it, they just figured we were going through some teenage phase. We spent a lot of time at an old bookstore we had found because it had a lot of books on the occult. It got to where we would just find things and follow the directions in the books. We were convinced that some of the magic, at least, was working. Our friend's family suddenly had to move because of work, so our coven went down to two, just myself and Rachel. The thing is that, once there were only two of us, things seemed to change. We didn't believe we were as powerful anymore and we didn't feel like the magic worked the same. The weird thing was, we always felt like someone else was in that little room with us. I started seeing a shadow form moving around the room. I thought maybe it was just due to the flickering of the candle flames because the shadows had that weird, jerky movement. But the shadows seemed to have a mind of their own. I could move the candles and the shadows wouldn't budge.

One night we did a ritual for one of the high Sabbaths. Rachel had to go home because she was leaving on a family trip early the next day. That night, the shadow forms were in my bedroom. I saw them come out of the closet and I knew they had come out from the hidden room. This started happening every night over the next several weeks. I would fall asleep, but wake up suddenly and they would be standing around my bed, staring at me. I tried everything I knew to try to banish them. I did protection techniques that I had learned in books but nothing worked. I couldn't find anything in my witchcraft books that would help."

Rebecca describes the shadow beings as small, around four feet in height. At any given time, there were three to five of them but she always had the sense there were more, hiding in the darkness or in the closet. Most disturbing, she said, was that the dark beings had glowing red eyes. She claims she was fully awake during the encounters, and as the experiences progressed, she had more difficulty sleeping even a portion of the night. At first, she started going down to the living room and sleeping on the couch. When questioned by her parents, she made the excuse that she had fallen asleep studying. This worked for a few days, but then she started seeing the shadow people in the living room too.

Rebecca came to believe it was her dabbling in the occult that allowed the beings to come through from the other side. She became convinced they were sprits of the deceased that wanted to make contact. Her attempts at reasoning with them or establishing a rapport were unsuccessful. Perhaps surprisingly, Rebecca did not abandon her practice of witchcraft and after she graduated high school, she moved in with a boyfriend who also practiced the craft. They both report that shadow beings are frequently in their home. They now believe the beings are inter-dimensional, and they are not human at all. They also believe that as long as the shadow people do not receive energy, they will not be capable of manifesting fully or causing harm to those in the physical world.

Rebecca's unique viewpoint and attitude towards the shadow people certainly places her in the minority. At this point, she even believes they are occasionally helpful. Is she serving her own ego or trying to avoid the responsibility of setting something loose in this world? Perhaps. Either way, she does not believe her role is to send them away but to merely keep them in check, a type of magical damage control.

"Yes, I believe I did something foolish and let this group of shadows in but I also believe that I can help keep them from fully coming into this world. It was my mistake, so now it's my responsibility to take care of the situation. We do things to keep them at bay and at least they're not off disturbing someone else. If anything happens to me, then other people in my coven will take over the work of holding these beings in their place."

Did Rebecca and her friend's practice of occult rituals open a doorway that allowed these beings to enter? Many magical systems teach the principle of opening passageways to other levels of existence, of calling out and connecting with spirits of the departed, or archetypes of higher beings. Such techniques employed by many people would probably be ineffective. Indeed, most teenagers quickly become bored with attempting such practices. In the perfect storm of emotions, energies and focus, however, it's possible the attempts of three teenage girls on this occasion forged a connection to some other place, some other level of reality that allowed something to slip through. If not this, then what exactly caused the emergence of these beings in the quiet North Carolina home? We may never know the answer, and we must hope Rebecca has made the right choice in her decision to keep watch over the group of little shadow beings in her home. Otherwise, there may be a new outbreak of activity in a sleepy Carolina town.

A Lingering Shadow

Countless theories have circulated to explain what the shadow beings actually are and where they come from. Popular theories include the belief they are the spirits of the dead. Trapped in some in-between level of existence, unable to fully manifest in the physical world, or, to move on to the afterlife. Some theories suggest the shadow people are the result of residual energy stored in a location for a long period of time. This would classify shadow people as a type of residual haunting, the result of a traumatic event or a sudden burst of emotional energy at the location at some point in the past.

Spiritually inclined people believe the shadows are demons or agents of evil working towards the destruction of those trying to lead spiritual lives. Others feel the shadow beings are from another dimension, crossing the void in an attempt to invade our world, gaining more energy and power with each visit. In this model, they are seen as the advanced guard of a race that intends to come to our level of existence for some nefarious purpose.

Still other theories posit the shadow people are elementals, beings of dark energy manifesting long enough to cause trouble and disrupt the lives of those unfortunate enough to notice them. Much like the archetypical trickster, they merely seek to disrupt for the pure joy of the chaos that ensues.

Another intriguing theory proposes the shadow beings are actually the manifestation of pure thought or negative energy. Like the classic Tulpa of Tibetan lore, these beings are a creation of concentrated energy, taking physical form and attempting to 'feed' on the energy of fear and dread they invoke in their victims. These types

31

of beings can eventually take on solid, physical form once they have taken a sufficient amount of energy. The issue however, is they still need to feed and their method for gaining energy is to gather it from the emotional output of humans.

In 2010, shadow people were listed as one of the most regularly reported types of paranormal phenomena in the United States. The number of reports has continued to skyrocket since then. Several factors may account for the growing number of reports. To some degree, the increase can be attributed to the dramatic rise in 'ghost hunting' teams across the nation. The popularity of paranormal reality television has led many people to pick up cameras and EVP (Electronic Voice Phenomena) recorders in an attempt to capture evidence of the afterlife. On any given night, teams across the country are investigating homes, businesses and historical locations in search of proof of spirits. Often, these teams encounter shadow people. Their reports fall in line with the common accounts given by those who deal with shadow beings in their daily lives—black figures, blacker than the darkness around them. Some are tall, some short. Some display the classic glowing eyes that victims have long reported. Some teams have captured EVP evidence they believe are the voices of shadow beings. At times, the shadow people seem to be curious about what the ghost hunters are doing, wondering perhaps why they are there and what all the electronic equipment is for. I've talked to teams around the country, and like most people, they are divided in their opinion as to what these beings are. Evil entities and spirits of the dead seem to be the most common opinions among paranormal groups.

Shadow people have been here in one form or another for a very long time. From phantom monks, to hat men, they have lurked in the shadows, casting an aura of malice and creating fear in their victims. By all appearances, whatever they are, they are here to stay.

Chapter Two From the Shadows

Chapter Three
Pukwudgies

The Troublesome Pukwudgies

Pukwudgies have a long history in southeastern Massachusetts. Well before the first colonists settled down in the states, natives told stories of the little creatures. In the early days of European settlement, the Pukwudgies were still a vital part of native traditions.

There are numerous spellings for the little creatures discussed in this chapter (e.g.,- Pukwasjineesuk, Pukwatcininins etc.) Most of the terms translate to mean "little people," "little man of the woods," or similar associations. For simplicity, I have used the spelling Pukwudgie pronounced, Pukwud-jie, a modern spelling often used when discussing the creatures.

It would be easy to dismiss the Pukwudgie as nothing more than a legend from the past. They do, after all, sound like a classical mythological creature, similar to the little people found in other cultures around the world. The Pukwudgies however, have never really vanished. Today, sightings and encounters continue to be reported on a regular basis. While the creatures have been reported in locations all over the northeast, some areas, such as the infamous Bridgewater Triangle, are hotspots for their activity.

A Pukwudgie is a small, troll-like creature, usually associated with the folklore of the Wampanoag Indians of Massachusetts. The creatures are between two and three feet tall. They resemble humans somewhat, but their features are exaggerated. They have thick hair on their bodies, large ears, oversized mouths, and oversized noses that sometimes look canine. Their fingers are long and their skin is usually described as being smooth and bluish-grey or ashen in color. Some accounts mention different colors, or even that they emit light, causing them to glow in the dark, but this may relate to some of their purported magical abilities. Their clothing, such as it is, is made of

35

material taken from nature, such as bark, limbs and leaves. This gives them a form of camouflage allowing them to blend in easily with the forest.

According to Native traditions, Pukwudgies are able to appear and disappear at will. They are able to use magic and can create fire. They have sticks, poison arrows and short knives. They are fond of using sand to blind their victims. They also possess a poison dust they will throw on people. Some accounts say they can transform into a porcupine-like creature that walks upright. Other legends claim the little people can shape shift into animals such as birds, dogs or even insects.

They are considered to be troublesome creatures. While some legends say the Pukwudgies were once friendly towards humans, they became trickster-like, and in many cases downright sinister. It is purported they are able to control the souls of people who they have killed, turning them into spirit lights called 'Tei-Pai-Wankas' which they use to lure in more innocent people. People find themselves compelled to follow these lights, which often lead them far off the beaten path. It is believed the Pukwudgies will lure people to rocks where they can crush them or towards cliffs where they can push them off to their deaths.

According to Native Americans, it is best to ignore the Pukwudgies, even if you see one. Acknowledging it, or paying any attention to it will only aggravate it and it will follow you, stirring up trouble and causing you misfortune at every opportunity. Iron, salt and reciting the Lord's Prayer are all considered useful defenses against the Pukwudgies.

Some of the prime locations for Pukwudgie encounters lie within the Bridgewater Triangle. The triangle is an area of about two hundred square miles in Southeastern Massachusetts. The points of the triangle are commonly listed as Abington, Freetown and Rehoboth. The Freetown State Forest lies within the boundaries of the triangle along with other notable locations such as Anawan Rock and the Hockomock Swamp. The Bridgewater Triangle was first defined by researcher and author Loren Coleman in his book *"Mysterious America."* Numerous towns fall within the triangle and countless types of paranormal phenomena have been reported in the area. Bigfoot sightings, UFOs, balls of light and ghostly activity are just the tip of the iceberg. The area is also known for suicides, satanic and cult activity, and ritual crimes. It would take pages and pages to even begin to document the area, and that is not my intent here. Author Christopher Balzano has published two excellent books on the Bridgewater Triangle. *"Ghost of the Bridgewater Triangle"* and *"Dark Woods,"* they are both recommended to those interested in this strange region.

Early Tales of the Pukwudgies

Pukwudgies are a part of the early stories of the Wampanoag Indians. The tale begins with a hero figure of the Wampanoag called Maushop. Maushop was a giant, believed to have created Cape Cod. He was loved by the Native Americans who lived in the region and hated by the Pukwudgies who constantly attempted to cause trouble. The Pukwudgies were jealous of the affection the natives had for Maushop and so they tried to be helpful to humans. Their true, trickster nature came through however, and they would inevitably change their minds and go back to causing mischief.

The natives were constantly tormented by the little people. In fact, the natives became so aggravated they called out to Maushop's wife, Squanit for help. Squanit went to her giant husband and demanded that he do something about the irritating creatures. Maushop went about and began collecting the Pukwudgies. He would gather them up and shake them hard until they were confused and dizzy. Then he would toss them away as far as he could, throwing them all across New England. Some died from the harsh treatment; others regained their senses and angrily made their way back to Massachusetts.

Satisfied the Pukwudgies would no longer be a problem, Maushop went away for awhile to rest. He was gone a long time and when he returned, he found the Pukwudgies had returned too. He also discovered their actions had become evil towards the native peoples. Pukwudgies were kidnapping children, luring adults into the forest to their deaths, and burning down the people's homes and villages. Maushop did not want to deal with the little people again, so he sent his five sons to take care of the problems with them. This time, the Pukwudgies were ready for the giants. The little creatures hid in the tall grasses and lured Maushop's sons into the marshes. There they fired magic arrows into the giants causing them to fall over. Maushop and Squanit were enraged by the attack on their children, they pursued the Pukwudgies and began to kill as many as they could. Some of them ran away, fleeing to different parts of

New England. Others banded together and tricked Maushop into the water. Once there, they began to shoot him with their poison arrows. Some versions of the tale claim the Pukwudgies were able to kill the giant and that his body fell, sinking into the depths of the water. Others say Maushop ran away, unable to defeat the powerful magic of the little beings. Either way, Maushop vanishes from the legends of the Wampanoag after this tale. The Pukwudgies however, remain.

Assawompset Pond

Assawompset Pond lies within the towns of Middleboro and Lakeville in southeastern Massachusetts. Measuring almost four square miles, Assawompset is the largest natural lake in the state and supplies drinking water for the city of New Bedford.

It was known to the Wampanoag as the "Place of the White Stones." Its name was derived from the abundance of quartz found in the area. Natives would use the quartz in their rituals, but it's also worth noting that quartz records energy, so it could certainly be a factor in the high amount of ghostly activity reported around the lake.

The lake is the location of the largest herring run on the eastern seaboard. During some seasons, the water is so thick with fish heading toward the spawning grounds, that it appears to turn black. Traditionally, the Native Americans would have a summer camp on the banks of the water, enjoying the bounty of fish. A dig was conducted between 1957 and 1959 in the woods near the Assawompset's north shore. Archaeologists uncovered the remains of one of the ancient native campsites. Stone tools and weapons were found, along with the charred remains of several people. Carbon testing dated the remains to about 2,300 B.C. Curiously, the dig was abandoned after three summers and no one seemed to know why further work was not done.

Assawompset pond is especially notable because of its connection to the origins of King Philip's War. John Sassamon was a 'praying Indian' a native who had converted to Christianity. In late 1674, Sassamon had warned the governor of the Plymouth colony that an attack by Metacomet, also known as King Philip, was imminent. The governor ignored the warning, believing the natives would not dare such an attack. Sassamon went missing and in early 1675, his body was discovered in Assawompset pond. His neck had been broken.

Another native convert to Christianity, a man known as Patuckson came forward and claimed he had seen three of Metacomet's men kill Sassamon and throw him in the icy water. The Puritans blamed Metacomet for the murder. They held a trial and convicted Metacomet's three warriors, then executed them. These events are generally believed to have been the spark that ignited the conflict known as King Philip's War.

Locals have long talked about odd, flickering lights that would appear at night in the woods on the lake's north shore. Others have claimed to see the ghosts of Native Americans around the water. Much of this activity began after the archaeology work was conducted. The strange lights, people would often say, appeared over the area where the dig took place. Perhaps something, or someone, had been disturbed.

Some legends say the pond is the final resting place of Maushop and his wife, killed in the battle with the Pukwudgies. Hundreds of the little people also perished in this legendary fight, killed by the native warrior and his wife. Fog rolling off the pond is said to be the smoke from Maushop's pipe. Some even believe the apparition of Maushop himself has appeared on the water. The pond has certainly long been associated with the little people. Thomas Weston in his book, *"History of the Town of Middleboro, Massachusetts"* published in 1906, says there was an island in Assawompset pond where the Pukwudgies lived. There are still sightings of the little troublemakers in the area.

Throughout the years, numerous people have reported seeing the mysterious lights around Assawompset pond. Some say they are the size of baseballs or even larger. They are purported to move about like fireflies in the night, sometimes diving down into the water, vanishing briefly, then reappearing suddenly. Perhaps these lights are the Tei-Pai-Wankas, the orbs of light controlled by Pukwudgies and used to lure people to their deaths. A local named Joe decided to take a couple of people out to the lake to see if they could spot the floating lights. He spotted more than he bargained for:

"We were out at Assawompset Lake. It was late spring and the weather was nice. We got there kind of late in the day and we were waiting for the sun to go down. For years, we had heard stories of strange lights that would appear and move around. We wanted to get a glimpse of them. My girlfriend was with me and so was her cousin, a guy named Chad. Chad claimed that he had seen the lights before when he was young. I wasn't sure if I believed they were real or not. Once the sun started going down we got anxious wondering if we would see something when it was finally dark. There was still plenty of light out, we probably had another half an hour or more before it would get dark enough for lights to show up. I was getting nervous though. I kept feeling like something was watching us. I sat down, then I got back up and paced around. My girlfriend was getting irritated with me but I couldn't shake the feeling, I couldn't get comfortable. Maybe another ten minutes had passed. I was walking around, we were in a little clear area. I thought I saw something move out of the corner of my eye. That made me really nervous. Then I saw it again. This time, I really saw it.

It was some kind of little man. He was about three feet tall. I only really saw him from the waist up because he was looking out from around a tree. It really freaked me out. The little man had wild hair that went in every direction. He had a big nose, large ears and a big mouth. He looked like he was really pissed off, maybe because I had seen him. I couldn't help myself; I let out a scream. I know it wasn't very manly, but it just happened. It seemed to anger the little man even more because he really scowled at me then. I turned and I ran. I passed my girlfriend and her cousin yelling that I was out of there and I kept going until I reached my car. I didn't know if they were following me or not, but either way I was leaving. I got in the car and started the engine. They were both jumping in the car as I put it into gear to leave. It turned out that seeing me so freaked out had scared them, too. Later I told them what had happened. Chad said that I had seen a Pukwudgie and that I would have a whole bunch of bad luck. Maybe it's true. It wasn't long after that I split with my girlfriend and then I had to move because my apartment building got sold. I'm not going back to that pond and I have no desire to ever see one of those evil little men again."

Assonet Ledge

Located in the Freetown State Forest, Assonet Ledge is purportedly the most haunted stone location in the forest. Many tragic deaths have occurred at the spot, including over a dozen suicides. Many people experience an overwhelming, deep sadness or dread at the location. At times there is an unexplainable urge to leap off into the water below — a jump that spells certain death. The ledge is home to a famous spirit known as the "Lady of the Ledge" along with phantoms of native warriors, spirits of early settlers, and, perhaps, Pukwudgies.

In the early 1900s, the site was used as a blacksmith shop and quarry. A tragedy occurred at the site when a quantity of dynamite exploded. Several men were killed in the explosion and the company was forced to shut down the entire operation. Perhaps the location itself is cursed as some Native Americans have suggested. A story passed around by some native people claims the whole area will be cursed until it is all returned to the Wampanoag. Most tribal members do not subscribe to this aspect of the tale; however, it is hard to deny there is a heaviness in the environment around the ledge itself. The geography of the area may be a factor in adding to the strange feelings experienced at the location. The landscape is comprised of granite, feldspar and hornblende. Combined with the area's running water, these components may be conducive to paranormal activity and unusual incidents.

There's a legend that surrounds the so-called Lady of the Ledge. The story says that a young woman was waiting to meet her lover at the ledge. Her beau's family was not happy with the young man's choice and refused to let him leave the house. Overwhelmed with sadness and believing her love had abandoned her, the young woman leapt off the ledge to her death. The intensity of her sadness caused her phantom to remain at the ledge, forever mourning the loss of her true love.

Even local authorities admit there have been a number of unexplained deaths and suicides around the ledge. There is speculation that the deep water below the ledge could conceal additional bodies, but conditions make it too difficult to explore the water in search of anyone lost there. Graffiti is also a frequent issue at Assonet Ledge. Teenagers who live nearby often use the location as a place to hang out, party and drink. They also notice the heavy, depressive energy in the rocks.

The spirits of Native Americans have often been reported around Assonet Ledge. Perhaps the strange feelings in the place run deep into the past. It has also become a location firmly associated with the infamous Pukwudgies. Christopher Balzano, writing in *"Ghosts of the Bridgewater Triangle"* says:

"People believe that the Pukwudgies have a hand in the hauntings at the ledge. It is known that they often lured people to rocks and cliffs and then pushed them over. While no one has ever spotted a creature at the spot, orbs and flashes of light, typical traits of the Pukwudgie, are often seen."

There have been many reports of ghostly lights seen at Assonet Ledge. As Balzano states, orbs are frequent, as are floating and flickering lights. Some people report seeing balls of light that drop down from the cliff and vanish into the water. Perhaps these are the Tei-Pai-Wankas, the lost spirits that the Pukwudgies control. Are the little people lurking about the ledge, waiting to push off unsuspecting visitors? If you visit, it's probably wise not to stand too close to the edge.

Pukwudgies in Indiana

The Pukwudgies are also reported outside of their home state of Massachusetts. There are accounts of them in New Hampshire, Maine and Rhode Island. There are also Pukwudgie stories from Indiana. Author Michael Newton lists a Pukwudgie account in his book, *"Strange Indiana Monsters."*

"In June 1927, while hiking along Indiana's White River, ten-year-old Paul Startzman found an abandoned gravel pit and there met a two-foot-tall man wearing a light blue robe. "We stood about ten yards apart and looked at each other," Startzman later said. "He had thick, dark blond hair, and his face was round and pinkish in color, like it was sunburned." After a moment, the tiny, barefoot figure turned and fled into the woods."

Startzman claimed he later had another meeting with the little man in the same area. Startzman had a friend with him during this second encounter and he reported the small man followed behind them for some time before vanishing among the trees. Startzman also talked to reporters about his encounter and it was noted the boy's mother was full-blooded Native American, perhaps indicating a connection to the little people through heritage.

Although this is the only account that Newton lists in his book, it is not the only Pukwudgie encounter to come out of the state of Indiana. Recent reports claim the little creatures are active around Mounds State Park in Anderson, Indiana. Located in the central part of the state, the park contains ten ceremonial mounds built by the prehistoric Adena culture. The area was later used by the Hopewell culture. There are many native legends around the park and its ancient mounds. Perhaps the Pukwudgies made their way to the location at some point, or maybe they have been there much longer than anyone realizes.

The Red Creatures at Vale End

Ghost Hunter and author Fiona Broome posted an account of her sighting of a Pukwudgie-like creature in the Vale End Cemetery of Wilton, New Hampshire. The events leading up to her encounter began in 1999. In November 1999, Broome and her team were investigating a cemetery on Gilson Road. After the investigation concluded, one of the team members told Fiona that she and her daughter would be stopping by Vale End Cemetery on their way home. It was close to their house and they wanted to take some more photographs before calling it a night.

The mother and daughter parked their car in the cemetery's lot and began walking around. Vale End was known as a haunted location with a legendary "Blue Lady" who was associated with a particular headstone. Walking towards the headstone, the investigator spotted something dark that appeared to rise up out of the ground. Something terrified the two women in that moment. The woman and her daughter fled the scene as rapidly as they could, speeding home, unsure of what they had experienced. Arriving at home, the woman called Fiona and related her experience, asking if it was possible she could have been followed home by the negative energy she had felt. Broome assured her that everything was okay.

The disturbing twist to this story is that five days later the woman was found sitting in her car in a busy parking lot, deceased. Doctors believed the cause of death was a heart attack. The woman was not very old and was in good physical condition, so the incident took friends and family completely by surprise. Obviously, such things happen, and there was no reason to connect it to the strange experience at the cemetery a few days prior.

It became a nagging question for Fiona Broome however, especially in light of her own experiences at Vale End Cemetery, which unfolded the following spring.

She and three other investigators were in the cemetery one night. The only notable activity was a high level of EMF (Electromagnetic field) readings near the Blue Lady's grave. Just as darkness began to fall, the group decided to end their investigation. Broome headed for the Blue Lady's headstone for one last round of photos. That's when she spotted what she referred to as "a little Grover guy." Recounting the incident on her Website, "Hollow Hill" she says:

"...I spotted what I've since called "a little Grover guy" about two or three feet from me...He was short, between two and three feet tall. He looked like he was covered with fur, and disproportionately skinny like Grover." (The popular puppet character from Sesame Street.) Broome notes the small figure was "a vivid shade of red." The ghost hunter was surprised but not bothered by the creature. She continued walking towards her destination. Right after this sighting however, Broome encountered an invisible force she believed was "something profoundly evil" and beyond this, she suddenly realized there were dozens of the small fur-covered creatures in the cemetery.

Determined to capture evidence of the creatures, Broome raised her camera and started snapping pictures. Her camera seemed to reveal more of the creatures.

"As I raised my camera and looked through the viewfinder, the red Grover guys seemed to multiply. When my camera clicked, I saw three of them clearly outlined by the flash."

Satisfied she had caught the beings on film, she suddenly had the strong impression she was in danger. She moved quickly to her car and left the area along with the other ghost hunters.

Later, when the film was developed, Broome discovered all of the shots she had taken were completely black with the exception of a single shot. In it, there was a red shape, the same vivid color as the creatures she had seen. Demonologist John Zaffis later correlated the strange image captured by the camera to a sign of demonic manifestation.

Despite having hundreds of ghost hunts under her belt, Fiona was genuinely frightened by her encounter in Vale End and says, in fact, it was the only time she's ever been frightened on an investigation. Never one to believe in demonic forces prior to the experience, Broome now considers the possibility of such evil entities. Her description of the small, furry figures falls within the general appearance of Pukwudgies although the red fur is unusual. Was this due to their connection to some demonic force? Legend says the little guys are able to shapeshift after all; perhaps they are also affected by energies that they align themselves with.

Broome says that on follow up trips to the Wilton area, she experienced the menacing feelings just as she had when she saw the little figures. This reaction continued for two years before stopping.

Other ghost hunters have reported similar experiences at Vale End Cemetery. One seasoned investigator told me he always had the sense of "something small running about, staying just out of direct view" when he was in Vale End. He would see blurs of red or grey in his peripheral vision. Other members of his team reported similar experiences. He even posted cameras at the location in an attempt to capture the creatures but his efforts only yielded blurred or blacked out images, nothing red like Broome's strange photo capture. "There's something in there," he told me, but after his last attempt, he became very ill with a stomach virus. "It lasted almost two weeks. I can't prove it's because I was in Vale End, but that's what I believe. I won't be going back," he stated.

As for Fiona Broome, she continues to work in the paranormal field writing, lecturing and investigating. She talked about her experience with the Vale End entities during her appearance at 2007's Dragon Con in Atlanta, Georgia, but otherwise, she is reluctant to speak about the incident. Despite the intensity of her encounter in Wilton, she prefers not to use the word demon:

"That's outside my field of study. I no longer scoff at the idea of demons. And, I stay far away from anything related to them."

Vale End used to be accessible and was a popular location for ghost hunting groups. In recent years however, the town began enforcing a strict rule closing the cemetery after dark. Police now patrol the location on a regular basis to ensure this restriction is not violated. For her part, Fiona Broome is relieved that the cemetery has become off limits to ghost hunters:

"I'm glad that the police patrol Vale End Cemetery steadily after dark, to prevent others from visiting it. And, I firmly recommend that no one go there for a ghost hunt."

Other Little Troublemakers

From Southeastern Canada to the Great Lakes region and all

the way across to California, legends of little people can be found all over North America. While the Pukwudgies are unique in their level of involvement in Wampanoag lore and their defeat of a hero figure, other little people are known to be trouble makers with slightly less influence.

Cherokee tales speak of several different types of little ones. Called Yunwi Djunsti, they are described as being between two and three feet tall and humanoid in form. They speak the same language as the Cherokee people and possess a social structure. The Yunwi Djunsit have long hair that often reaches the ground and they wear white clothing. They are usually invisible to humans and have the ability to hear anything said about them.

The Cherokee identified four different types of these little beings. Some live in the mountains, in hard to reach crags and rocks. Others live in rhododendron patches. These two are considered to be generally helpful to humans as long as they are not mistreated. The third type live in scrub brush and the last live out in the open. These final two are considered untrustworthy and troublesome. They will trick people when given the opportunity and they like to wreak havoc when possible. It is considered bad luck to see these little creatures and they are believed to be omens of death. Like the Pukwudgies, the Yunwin Djunsti are known for luring travelers off the path, sending them deep into the mountains. They will also lure children away from their parents, or abduct them from homes.

Another malicious figure is the Mannegishi, known to the Cree people. These beings are humanoid creatures, two to three feet tall. They are thin and lanky with long arms and legs. Their heads are oversized and they have no nose. The Cree say these little beings are nasty tricksters. They live among the rocks in rapids and take great joy in popping up and overturning canoes of those trying to travel the waters where they live.

Are the Pukwudgies a mere legend from the times when Native Americans ruled over the land? Are they just fanciful stories that cause the imagination to run wild when people are deep in the forest or visiting the rocky crags of the northeast? From traditional tales, we can see the Pukwudgies are masters of survival, despite difficult conditions and adversity. It's possible these little creatures have found a way to coexist in the ever-changing world, adapting even while the world closes in around them. Perhaps that quick moving figure out of the corner of your eye *is* something more than imagination.

Strange Intruders | *David Weatherly*

Chapter Four
Mummies, Monkey Men and Bizarre Attacks

Bizarre Attackers

In the annals of fortean lore, we find cases of strange figures, questionably human, that appear suddenly, carry out a series of bizarre attacks, and then disappear. Monkey men, mad gassers, oily men and of course, the infamous Spring-heeled Jack all fall into this category. Who or what are these creatures? Aliens? Crazed scientists? Perhaps a government experiment gone awry?

The skeptics would say, and have said, that most of these cases are the result of mass hysteria. There was no monkey man, the mad gasser didn't exist, it was all a grand figment of the imagination. That is, hundreds of people in any given case were imagining these things. Apparently, the "rational thinkers" believe we're all on the verge of suffering an outbreak of madness and mass hysteria at any given moment.

Truthfully, some of them are most likely nothing but humans (I won't call them normal) who have strange fetishes, ideas and desires. Other cases are likely the result of clever criminals, attempting to capitalize on myths, legends and primal fears in order to catch people off guard and take advantage. These attackers leave little behind to help authorities determine what they're dealing with. But all too often, there seem to be questions hanging that remain unanswered. Why do these attackers suddenly appear and just as suddenly end their reign of terror and vanish into the pages of weird history?

Some would opt for these beings having a supernatural origin, the result of magic and mystical practices. Perhaps they traveled here through some hole in the fabric of our reality, slipping in to wreak havoc for a time before leaving via the same route.

You may think yourself safe in a small town, but, alas, rural areas are no safer from these weird characters than large metropolitan centers are, as you will discover in this chapter. Phantom attackers can appear anywhere, perhaps it's completely random or maybe these villains choose their locations very specifically, we'll never be sure, but when they do turn up, it's sure to be an interesting and creepy time.

The Fairfield Mummy

Cypress, Texas is a quiet town northwest of Houston. In January 2011, in the Fairfield area of Cypress, residents were dealing with an unusual problem. There was a mummy prowling the neighborhood.

According to Houston's KPRC news, Fairfield area residents were "living in fear" since the figure, described as a mummy, had started running about the quiet suburban neighborhood. Cypress homeowner Jon Hill called the police after he spotted the strange entity moving around the front yard of his home on Chestnut Falls Drive. According to Hill the being had:

"Bandages, like a mummy. He looked like a mummy. It's scary not knowing what this man is up to or what he wants."

Numerous people have spotted the mummy on more than one occasion. The Harris County sheriff's department advised residents to call 911 immediately if they spotted the creepy character. Authorities were convinced the figure was merely a man dressed as a mummy but were unsure about his motives.

Area resident Steven Scheiffele echoed the feelings of many in his neighborhood:

"It's creepy, especially since he's here in the neighborhood with the kids and stuff."

Malaysia's Terrible Oily Man

It's a Christmas weekend in the Kampung district of Malaysia. At well after midnight, around 200 people are patrolling the streets armed with machetes, axes and sticks. This is not a riot or gang related violence, these citizens are determined to defend the neighborhood's innocent young women from the dreaded "Orang Minyak" or "Oily Man".

The orang minyak, or oily man, has long been a part of Malaysian lore. Some believe these creatures are supernatural beings involved in dark magic and evil practices. Others believe they're simply criminals or sexual deviants prowling the village. Either way, residents are eager to put a stop to the fear the oily man has created.

The oily man is described as being human in form, clad only in black underwear with his body drenched in black, shiny oil.

There are a few different versions of the oily man legend. One says the creatures are humans who have turned to the practice of black magic. These practitioners are required to go through certain rites of passage in order to complete a course of learning in the dark arts. For the magical knowledge to be useful and complete, the practitioner is supposed to rape a certain number of virgins. The number of virgins varies according to the teacher or demon imparting the knowledge. Some say the number is forty, others say it is ninety-nine. The oily man is given the ability to recognize virgins on sight to facilitate this requirement.

Once mastered, the black arts impart a wide range of abilities to the orang minyak. These powers include the ability to walk through walls and vanish into thin air. The orang minyak can gain strength by sucking water from a banana bud. They are purported to have amazing agility, far beyond that of a normal human, enabling them to leap great distances with ease. Their magic, along with the oil on their bodies, allows them to escape any trap with ease.

In Kampung, residents believe two orang minyak are on the prowl. Tension is high as the village men search the streets for this disturbing figure. Reports say the oily man usually attacks between the hours of midnight and four AM. Few of the residents are getting much sleep, those not on patrol sleep clustered together for safety, leaving the lights on for additional protection.

Numerous area residents claim to have seen and/or heard the creatures in their village. They all say the oily men are clad only in underwear and drenched in black, shiny oil, as the legends say. A local man, P. Mohan, saw one of the creatures on the house across from his flat at about twelve-thirty one night. He told a reporter:

"It was crawling up the stairs of the house, just like Spiderman. When it reached the top it suddenly jumped onto the roof. I don't think a human could do that. It then just disappeared. The hair on my hands just stood up. We can laugh and joke about it but this is serious. All the families here have young girls."

One of the nightly patrols spotted an oily man and gave chase. They lost him in the bushes, but they came across a spot they believe was a ritual area for one of the creatures. On the ground was a large patch of oil, some believe one of the orang minyak stood and bathed in his ritual oil while reciting magical mantras. Returning to check the same spot the next night, the patrol found fried rice and noodles. Returning later the same night, they discovered the food was gone, eaten by the orang minyak before his nightly endeavors began, or so the patrol believes.

All of this likely sounds preposterous to the Western 'educated' mind. Indeed, many people who live in the region even believe that the orang minyak is simply a wild tale of the imagination. Sightings of the oily men have cropped up in Malaysia over the last several decades. Some of the accounts can be dismissed as mistaken identity, overreaction due to fear, and of course, real human beings committing crimes.

The oily man legend became more widespread in Malaysia with the release of the 1956 film, "Sumpah Orang Minyak" or, "The Curse of the Oily Man." The movie was directed by P. Ramlee who also starred in the film. In this version the orang minyak is a normal man, cursed in an attempt to win back his love through the use of dark magic. The devil himself offers the man the powers of black magic in return for his worship. In addition, the cursed man is required to sexually assault twenty-one virgins within a week's time.

Not surprisingly, the film led to more oily men stories, and by the 1960s numerous towns in Malaysia were reporting sightings and encounters with orang minyak. Much like the legend, the men were reported to be almost naked and covered in black oil. Stories at this time claim the creature was invisible to anyone who was not a virgin. Some areas saw near-panic among unmarried women. Female college students began to borrow sweaty clothing from male friends that they could leave in their quarters, leading to the appearance they had been with a man to deter the orang minyak. Other supposed defenses against the creature were biting its left thumb if it tried to attack, or covering it in batik.

Sightings and reports continued well beyond the movie's initial run. Every few years, it seemed, there was an outbreak of oily man accounts that turned up. The frequency of these accounts slowed down by the 2000s, but in 2005 there was again another rash of sightings. Some of these cases turned out to be human rapists who had covered themselves in oil, attempting to ply on the fears of the orang minyak legend.

The outbreak of 2012 among the residents of Kampung was a bit different. Countless reports were submitted and there is no denying the genuine fear and concern the village was experiencing.

"It's definitely no laughing matter," stated Aslam Khan, thirty-three. Khan is one of the Kampung villagers who spotted a pair of oily men roaming the streets. According to Khan's description, one of the men was tall, stocky and bald while the other was thin with curly hair. Khan recounts:

"I saw the bald orang minyak behind the water tank of a house at about two in the morning. It was breathing really loudly, like a cow. It was black and shiny. When I shone my light on it, the thing stuck out its head to look back at me. Before I could do anything, it climbed up the roof and disappeared. Until we manage to catch this thing, we are going to carry on with our patrols. I don't feel calm, although I don't have a wife or younger sister."

A Malaysian daily newspaper, *The Star* reported that a seventeen-year-old girl had seen an orang minyak several times and that she had felt someone caress her and call for her to leave the house. The creature reportedly locked family members out of their home on Christmas Eve, forcing Kamal Bahari Satar to break down the door. When the family entered the house, they saw a strange sight:

"We saw a black heap underneath the kitchen table. When other residents poked it with a bamboo stick, we could see bloodstains. It then fled to a neighbor's house."

Kamal told *The Star* disturbances continued in the home in the following days, forcing the man to move his family out of the house and out of the neighborhood.

Muaz Amran, twenty-one, who takes part in the nightly patrols, says he never believed in such things before the incidents:

"I thought the thing existed only in the movies but it seems to be happening in real life."

Another resident of the village says he was woken on Christmas day at three AM by a commotion outside his home:

"Apparently, the orang minyak had run into the next-door neighbor's house but I just brushed aside the incident." The man who is a bank official, says his niece, a university student, saw the oily man the next night. He was sitting on the wall outside of a house. "She woke up when she heard something. When she peeked out of the window, she saw a black figure sitting on the wall with its back facing her."

Residents say it has become difficult to rest even in groups with the lights on. People are nervous, jumping at the slightest sound and no one has any peace of mind. To date, the Kampung oily men have not been caught. While some are convinced it's another case of common criminals and rapists trying to strike fear by using old legends, others are convinced the creatures have a supernatural source. Until these two are caught, the matter will remain a mystery.

Chaotic Days of the Monkey Man

May 2001, New Delhi, India. It's past midnight, the sun has been down for hours, but still the heat is stifling and unbearable. Rolling blackouts plague the city, so there are often no lights, air conditioning or fans — nothing for relief from the high temperatures. Hoping to catch the cool night air, people sleep outside, on balconies and rooftops.

Suddenly the darkness is pierced by screams and there is panic. People push and yell in a mad attempt to get inside to safety. Amid the chaos, a pregnant woman falls down a flight of stairs. She later dies from her injuries.

India is in the grip of the Monkey Man.

It is described as being four feet tall, covered in thick black hair or fur. It wears a metal helmet on its head; some claim there are flashing green lights on the helmet. Others say the flashing lights are on the creature's chest where three buttons flash different colors. Its eyes are flaming red or perhaps like a cat's eyes with a strange glow. The creature has fierce metal claws that it uses to lash out at its victims.

These, and many other details, continued to pour into police in the days and weeks that followed the initial report. Some accounts and details were in conflict with others. Police received hundreds of complaints of the Monkey Man. Countless claims of attacks, bites and scratches were logged in at police headquarters.

Skeptics claim the wounds have nothing to do with supernatural beings and are merely self-inflicted, or the result of panicked people running about in the darkness.

Sanal Edammaruku, head of India's "Rationalist Association," a group of skeptics, attempts to explain the situation thus:

"When wild fears are at a pathological level, critical faculties disappear and gullibility gains control."

Sanal and others believed the Monkey Man attacks were nothing but a result of fantasy and mass hysteria.

What is not fantasy however, are the tragic deaths of several people during the attacks. A man leapt from a rooftop late one night in sheer terror. As he fell to his death, neighbors were chilled by his final words, "The Monkey has come!"

The Monkey Man attacks started in Ghaziabad, a small township twenty-two miles north of New Delhi. Early reports described the creature as an exceptionally large monkey around five feet tall. People claim the creature attacks without provocation, scratching with its large claws and biting the neck of sleeping victims. Ganesh Jha of the Maharana Vihar Residents Association came face-to-face with the Monkey Man. He gave his account to reporters:

"We were taking an evening walk when we walked into this huge man-monkey. The monster sprang up twenty feet from a crouching position and grabbed branches of a tree and vanished before me and my children could even scream."

As the number of reported encounters with the monkey man grew, descriptions became more varied. He was black, white or reddish brown. He was half human, or perhaps half feline. His eyes glowed red or maybe orange. Perhaps it was simply a man wearing a costume and a mask. Anim Keshri, a thirty-five year old shopkeeper thought the monkey man was some kind of robot, manipulated by remote control. "How else could it leap four stories and disappear?"

By May 14, the area of the reported attacks had spread and

accounts were coming from a number of areas in East Delhi. It was an especially busy night for the Monkey Man, as according to the newspaper, *"The Australian,"* over fifty attacks were reported.

The mood in New Delhi quickly changed. Children were afraid to play outside for fear the monkey would come. Bands of vigilantes began to patrol the streets at night. Armed with sticks they sought to defend their communities and perhaps claim the 50,000-rupee reward offered by the police for the monkey man's capture.

The police department set up a special investigation unit to deal with the case. They released a computer-generated sketch showing two different versions of the creature. It was widely circulated by the media and served to fuel the panic that already gripped the city. Police officers were posted on rooftops for added protection. Despite the power cuts, many areas were kept well lit from dusk to dawn. Checkpoints were set up at the city's various points of entry, an assurance against any foreign agents that would try to take advantage of the city's troubles. The *"Daily Pioneer"* interviewed police officials on May 16 and received this statement from a senior officer:

"The whole drama was very carefully enacted by the anti-social elements who wanted to test the nerves of the Delhi Police."

Police officials implied the blame should be placed on Pakistan's Inter-Services Intelligence Agency. Indeed, India's archenemy Pakistan was a popular scapegoat for the attacks with claims they had trained monkeys and sent them across the border to harass India's citizens. Another theory proposed Pakistan had built a robot in the form of a monkey and controlled it remotely, all to wreak havoc on India's capital. *The Hindustan Times* promoted the mechanical Monkey Man and offered advice to those who might encounter it:

"Shining a light on it to scare it away, its night vision glasses become ineffective. You could also rob it of its gymnastic powers by throwing water on its chest, the creature's motherboard heart, concealed beneath its thick black coat of hair gets short-circuited."

Meanwhile, the range of the weird creature continued to expand. By May 17, calls reporting Monkey Man incidents were coming from countless areas of the city. Spreading panic brought more tragedies. In the suburb of Noida, a four-foot tall Sadhu (wandering holy man) was beaten up when an angry mob mistook him for the creature. He was turned over to the police, fortunately still alive. A van driver suffered a similar attack on May 18, sustaining multiple fractures from the mob that attacked him. In the early morning hours, he had been mistaken for the Monkey Man.

Throughout the chaos of the Monkey Man reports, countless theories continued to be presented in an attempt to explain the creature. Reports had continued to change, some now said the Monkey Man was eight feet tall, and was perhaps India's version of North America's Bigfoot. Its powerful body, they said, allowed it to leap from building to building with ease. Some believed there were whole gangs of monkey men running amok, terrorizing Delhi's citizens. Still others went a few steps in a different direction, noting the similarities to the Hindu God, Hanuman. Was the Monkey Man an avatar of the Monkey God? Perhaps Hanuman was unhappy and had sent his avatar into the night to frighten the people and send them towards a more spiritual path.

In June of 2001, the attacks stopped as suddenly as they had begun. Police officials claimed the entire affair was simply the result of mass hysteria and dismissed the case altogether. The media, without any further fuel, moved on to other topics and the Monkey Man faded from the headlines. Some people were still afraid and were cautious at night, feeling that the Monkey Man was still out there, haunting the rooftops in the late hours.

More Monkey Business

A year after the chaos in Delhi, a new wave of Monkey Man encounters began to surface. Located on the banks of the Ganges River, the city of Patna was the scene of one spate of accounts. This eastern city lies 360 miles southwest of New Delhi, but the Monkey Man reports were similar in nature to those that struck the capital. Residents reported their Monkey Man was able to make great leaps and sparkled red and blue lights when he jumped. Patna's chief of police, O.N. Bhaskar, issued a statement discouraging residents from spreading rumors about the supposed creature:

"There are rumors of a monkey-like machine, referred to as Monkey Man that attacks those sleeping on rooftops and in open places at night. But it is pure rumor as no one has actually lodged a case in any police station. There has not been any recognized case of injury. We have warned the public at large to be on guard against any rumor and help cops arrest those who spread such rumors."

The statement did little to help area residents feel safe, nor did it end talk of the Monkey Man. While police reports may not have been filed, people had no problem giving their accounts to reporters for the local newspapers. One resident, Bhagwat Sharan Singh stated:

"The Monkey Man attacked and injured my son-in-law Joginder Singh friday night when he was sleeping on the rooftop of my house. He (the attacker) looked like a monkey."

Like the New Delhi flap, Monkey Man attacks came to a sudden end in Patna and the creature vanished.

There were more eruptions of Monkey Man frenzy around India. The creature showed up again in February 2002 in Kanpur and in the summer of that year, he returned to New Delhi.

In February 2012, police once again had to deal with a panic concerning a Monkey Man. The story unfolded this time in Mumbai where residents began fearing a cannibal Monkey Man. They claimed the creature was leaping from rooftops into homes, raping women and then consuming them. This Monkey Man was also accused of kidnapping children. Some even began to fear a whole gang of these creatures existed, or perhaps a normal human gang was out to kidnap children for the underground slave trade. It all added up to a wave of fear and near panic. The rumors became so widespread some schools told parents not to allow their children to travel to or from school alone. Some parents kept their children home rather than risk their safety. Police responded rapidly in an attempt to quell the rumors. *The Hindustan Times* reported on police efforts to calm area citizens:

"There is no such gang or Monkey Man in the city. We request people not to panic as the city and its residents are safe," said Nisar Tamboli, spokesman for the Mumbai police.

Three children went missing in Kurar, fueling rumors of a gang of thugs applying heavy grease to their bodies and stealing children. The missing youngsters were later found in their homes, but the rumors were in full force. Other areas picked up on the story and soon Kurla, Chembur, Andheir, Ghatkopar and other villages were buzzing about monkey men and greasy gangs.

Tamboli further stated no one had actually seen the Monkey Man or the supposed gang, despite a number of misleading videos that had been posted, apparently, to fuel the rumors.

In recent years, the Monkey Man has become a part of popular culture and entertainment in India, appearing in movies, television and novels. The Monkey Man's activity in Old Delhi is at the core of an Hindi film, "Delhi-6" directed by Rakeysh Omprakash Mehra. In the Bollywood film, the creature is dubbed "Kala Bandar" (black monkey). In the storyline, the black monkey creature represents the essence of evil that resides inside every human alongside the essence of God.

The 2011 graphic novel, "Munkeeman" by Tere Bin Landen portrayed the creature as a misunderstood superhero attempting to do good. In this version, the Monkey Man is the result of a bizarre science experiment gone awry. Volume one of the series chronicled the Monkey Man's appearances in Delhi. A planned second volume of the series will be based on the Monkey Man's activity in Kanpur in February 2002.

Sporadic reports of the Monkey Man will probably continue to pop up across India leaving people afraid and puzzled. It may be explained as deranged criminals, strange robotic monkeys or an avatar of Hanuman. Perhaps people will suspect Pakistan is up to its old tricks again, or some other strange, unknown animal has come from the wild to wreak havoc. Either way the sightings will come, and most likely suddenly stop, leaving all to wonder what exactly it was in their midst.

Singapore's BTM

Singapore also has its own Monkey Man. Known as the Bukit Timah Monkey Man, the creature is often referred to by the initials BTM. The BTM is said to inhabit the forested region of Bukit Timah, and all of the known sightings have been centered in this area. The area is fairly small, just over four-hundred acres in size and surrounded by urban development, making an undiscovered species unlikely.

Many experts believe sightings of the BTM are simply a result of mistaken identity, noting the presence of large crab-eating Macaques that live in the region's rainforest. Other experts rely on the standard, favorite explanation of mass hysteria. Descriptions of the creature place it between three and six feet in height, bipedal and grey in color. The earliest recorded sighting of the creature dates to 1805 when a Malay elder reported encountering an upright humanoid with a monkey face walking in the Bukit Timah area. Further reports surfaced during World War II from Japanese soldiers who encountered the BTM. Sightings and rumors of the creature have continued into the 2000s with the most recent report in 2007. Singapore's Tabloid, *"The New Paper"* did a feature on the BTM that included several eyewitness reports. Included in the article, a 65-year-old retiree spoke of his childhood memories of the creature:

"We were always told as children when in the Kampung not to go near the forest at night due to the Monkey Man. Of course we never saw it ourselves but it was always some uncle or friend of the family who had seen it. Once, we were shown these footprints near the forest road, and I remember the strong urine smell. Whenever we heard shrieks coming from the jungle we would tell each other - don't disturb the Monkey Man."

In 2008, Chinese language newspaper *"Shin Min Daily"* featured the BTM, describing it as having the face of a monkey, but walking upright like a man. The Daily even went so far as to send a reporter to look for evidence of the creature. Alas, he returned from his explorations empty-handed.

Gassers

On the scale of strange attackers, gassers rate pretty high. These figures have the odd fixation of spraying chemicals with some type of device in order to incapacitate their victims. The most famous of these weird figures was known as the "Mad Gasser of Mattoon" or simply as the Mad Gasser, a character who was generally described as a tall, thin man dressed in dark clothing and wearing a tight fitting cap. Some people reported that he carried a flit gun, an agricultural tool used to spray pesticides. Supposedly, the mad gasser used this tool to emit his trademark gas into unsuspecting homes. But he wasn't the original gasser running about the states, that honor belongs to the villain that plagued rural Virginia in the 1930s.

The Botetourt Gasser

The earliest documented cases of this "gasser" occurred between December 1933 and February 1934 in Botetourt County, Virginia. Cal

Huffman and his family reportedly suffered three attacks by a gasser in the course of a single night. Huffman, of Haymakertown, reported a strange smell and a sudden feeling of nausea on the night of December 22, 1933. The first incident was at about ten o'clock at night but the odor and uneasy feeling soon passed. A half hour later, the odor and queasiness returned, prompting Huffman to contact the police. By one o'clock that night, another wave of the foul odor moved in, this time it went throughout the home, affecting eight Huffman family members and a guest. Those affected reported headaches, nausea and swelling as well as difficulties with constriction in the throat and mouth.

The Virginia gasser next struck on Christmas Eve at the home of Clarence Hall. Returning from a church service at nine o'clock, the family detected a strong odor in their home. They were rapidly overcome with weakness and nausea and contacted the police. Officers found that a nail had been removed from a window at the rear of the home, the area where the gas was generally concentrated.

A few days later on December 27, a Mr. Kelly of nearby Troutville suffered the next attack of nausea-producing gas. Police later learned that a neighbor had written down the partial license plate number of a 1933 Chevrolet that had been seen driving back and forth in front of the Kelly residence. A man and woman were spotted in the car, but no further information surfaced and the police were unable to track the vehicle.

A couple of quiet weeks followed before the gasser returned. Perhaps he needed to resupply or maybe he had taken off for the holidays. Either way, he struck again on January 10 at the home of Homer Hylton near Haymakertown. Homer and his wife were asleep in an upstairs bedroom. A Mrs. Moore, their older daughter, was staying with them at the time and was sleeping in a bedroom downstairs. She got up at ten o'clock to attend to her baby when she heard voices mumbling outside, along with a noise as if someone was messing with a window. According to Mrs. Moore, a moment later, the room filled with gas. She grabbed her baby just as she started to feel numb. A window in the Hylton household had been broken for some time and it was believed that the gasser took advantage of the break in order to inject gas into the home. The Hylton's neighbor, G.E. Poage, also reported hearing voices outside at the same time as the incident.

A long string of sporadic incidents unfolded in Botetourt County. Most of the reports were very similar in nature with residents reporting a strong smell, sometimes with a sickly-sweet odor. The gas quickly produced various reactions in the victims that commonly included nausea, headaches and difficulty in breathing. On some occasions, women's footprints were found in suspicious locations but few clues were found to help police determine anything about the gasser. After an attack at the home of Howard Crawford, officers found the crank of an old automobile — a strange item to be found, but nothing that could help police in their search.

January 22 brought three separate gasser attacks, all in the space of an hour, in Carvin's Cove. The gasser covered a distance of two miles, attacking the homes of Ed Reedy, George C. Riley and Raymond Etter. All of the victims suffered nausea and numbness. One of Etter's sons spotted a figure fleeing the home and gave chase, firing some shots in the process. The gasser eluded him however.

On January 23, the Hartsell family returned to their home late at night to find it filled with gas. To add to the strangeness, wood and brush had been piled against the outside of the front door. It is assumed the gasser was trying to prevent the family from escaping his foul concoction.

Men began patrolling the streets and keeping firearms close by. Other incidents were reported and some local farmers took potshots at suspicious figures. The Roanoke Times published a plea to residents to lay down their arms before an innocent person was shot. Concerned citizens began to stay with friends and relatives, seeking safety in numbers. The police seemed unsure about how to catch the gasser.

On January 28, the home of Ed Stanley in Cloverdale was attacked. Stanley and several other adults in the house were affected by the gas but one man, a farmhand named Frank Guy, managed to run outside at the first whiff of gas. He spotted four men running away from the house, headed towards the Blue Ridge Mountains. Guy dashed inside and retrieved a firearm but when he made it back outside, the men were nowhere in sight. Hearing them moving through the woods, Guy fired in the direction of their voices but did not manage to hit any of them.

Apparently, the gasser had it out for someone in the Stanley home because he attacked the house again two nights later. This time, Ed Stanley heard noises outside his window before the gas was injected. No further information about the Stanley incident is on record.

The final attack that seemed to be a genuine part of the Boutetourt gasser's spree took place on February 3 at the home of A.P. Skaggs. Seven adults, several children and even a dog, were victims of the gas. The dog reacted very strangely, running outside and rolling over and over in the snow as though he had been sprayed by a skunk.

There were other attacks over the following week but most of them are believed to be either pranks or mistaken reactions to common odors. Police were never able to solve the mystery of the Boutetourt gasser and the attacks simply ended, leaving a mystery for the quiet community to talk about for many years.

The Mad Gasser of Mattoon

A few years later, the gasser resurfaced, or perhaps it was a different gasser altogether. Either way, this one took up residence in Mattoon, Illinois. The year was 1944. The United States was still at war and many people were hoping for the conflict to end soon so their loved ones could return home. The quiet town of Mattoon, Illinois lies in the southeastern part of Central Illinois. This typical Midwestern town was to become the scene for a bizarre series of attacks that would forever leave their mark on the area.

In the early morning hours of August 31, Urban Raef was roused from his sleep by an odd odor. His nausea rapidly led to vomiting and weakness. Raef's wife found herself partially paralyzed and unable to rise from the bed. Later that night, in a nearby home, a woman and her daughter also succumbed to a strange gas that produced similar symptoms.

This particular gasser wasted no time in his operations. The next morning he attacked the Kearney home on Marshall Avenue. Mrs. Kearney was at home spending some time with her sister who was visiting. Kearney smelled an odor and suddenly started losing sensation in her legs. Her sister contacted the police who, arriving at the scene, could find nothing amiss. By mid-day, Kearney's husband, Bert, had returned to the home. When he reached the house, he spotted a prowler hiding below a window outside. The man ran away when he realized that Kearney had spotted him. Bert chased the man but soon lost him. Bert described the man as tall, thin and attired in dark clothes. The man wore a tight fitting cap so Kearney was unable to get a better look at his face. The account was published in local papers and the description became the common concept for the gasser.

Numerous attacks followed the Kearney incident. Again, the reports matched the standard gasser attack, strange odors, nausea, weakness, and sometimes vomiting and paralysis. While other people reported the prowler, no one, it seemed, could get a clear look at the gasser's face or come up with a better description than the rough one given by Bert Kearney.

Police were unsure exactly how to pursue the gasser. On September 5, they were given a physical clue. Carl and Beulah Cordes returned home that evening and found a scrap of white cloth sitting on their porch next to the door. When Beulah picked the cloth up to inspect it, she was overwhelmed by a strange odor. She felt a rough burning in her mouth and began to vomit. Her face and lips swelled and her mouth began to bleed. It took two hours for the symptoms to subside. The Cordes' suspected the cloth had been placed on the porch in order to knock out the family dog. As if this was not strange enough, other items were also found at the scene. A large tube of partially used lipstick was on the sidewalk next to the porch, along with a skeleton key that appeared to have been used extensively. Police believed the prowler had attempted to break into the home but was unsuccessful. Officials had the white cloth analyzed but could find no chemical trace of whatever had overwhelmed Beulah Cordes. Mrs. Cordes was interviewed by a local paper and stated:

"When I inhaled the fumes from the cloth, I had a sensation similar to coming in contact with an electric current. The feeling raced down my body to my feet, and seemed to settle in my knees. It was a feeling of paralysis."

Papers dubbed the gasser "The Mad Anesthetist" and began to publish sensational accounts of his attacks. As the attacks increased, the gasser seemed to get bolder. The same night the Cordes' found the odd collection of items at their home, another woman, Mrs. Leonard Burrell, reported a man breaking into her bedroom window and attempting to spray her with gas.

Concerned citizens began to form residential patrols, hoping to do the job the police had been unable to accomplish and capture the gasser. Local law enforcement attempted to assure the town they had everything under control, urging people to disband their patrol groups. In the midst of this, the FBI became involved. Two agents were called from Springfield to help solve the mystery, and hopefully help calm the citizens down. FBI, police, even armed patrols of concerned citizens did nothing to deter the gasser and his attacks continued.

Mrs. Violet Driskell and her daughter Ramona were attacked late one evening. They heard someone outside the bedroom window removing the storm sash, and they rushed out of bed to escape the house. Ramona fell, vomiting and overwhelmed by the gas before she could make it outside. Violet told police she witnessed a man running away from her home when she got outside.

Numerous other attacks took place in the following days. At the height of this excitement, a number of bizarre reports were made. One person claimed they had seen the gasser wearing a metal helmet; another believed the gas was the work of a mad scientist. Theories were tossed about left and right. It was a government experiment, it was the work of a Nazi agent, or perhaps aliens were involved. Many thought it was the work of an escaped mental patient.

Suddenly, it seemed the gasser was everywhere. Any footprint could be evidence; any slight sound outside the window could be the gasser lurking about waiting to spray his foul concoction. One report mentioned the sound of a motorized gassing machine and people began to speculate as to just what the villain was capable of. Finally, by September 12th the police had heard enough. Perhaps it was the panicked state of the people; perhaps they were frustrated at the local newspapers taking them to task for not capturing the gasser. These things, combined with the countless reports they were receiving, many of them mistakes and false alarms, prompted officials to issue a statement about the mad gasser. They blamed the entire affair on hysteria and anxiety, brought on by women who were upset so many local men were off fighting World War II. This explanation conveniently neglected to mention many of the victims were men and physical evidence had been found at many of the crime scenes.

The attacks continued, with a string of incidents in Mattoon and its outskirts. Public officials seemed to begin to contradict each other in their approach to the gasser incidents. Thomas V. Wright, Commissioner of Public Health, asserted that he did believe there had been some gassing incidents that were valid, but he attributed most of the accounts to hysteria. Wright stated:

"There is no doubt that a gas maniac exists and has made a number of attacks. But many of the reported attacks are nothing more than hysteria. Fear of the gasman is entirely out of proportion to the menace of the relatively harmless gas he is spraying. The whole town is sick with hysteria and last night it spread out into the country."

The Chief of Police, C.E. Cole, on the other hand, believed there wasn't a gasser at all and all of the incidents were hysteria combined with a chemical leak from the nearby industrial facility. Panic, he thought, led to wild stories and imaginings. Cole insisted the chemical carbon tetrachloride, or possibly trichloroethylene, was the source for the gas incidents. Both chemicals have a sweet odor and can cause symptoms akin to those reported by the gasser's victims. The gas had simply been carried on the wind, and it could account for stains that had been found on cloth. With the police chief's insistence the entire affair had been "...a mistake from beginning to end..." even the newspapers started to take a skeptical tone about the gasser.

Chief Cole's announcement really didn't sit well with people. Victims of the gasser, especially those who had seen a prowler lurking about, still wanted him caught. The Atlas-Imperial Diesel Engine Company, who Cole had implicated, released their own statement to the public. They reported they did indeed have carbon tetrachloride at their plant, but only five gallons of it for firefighting. The chemical, they assured the public, was safely stored away and had not leaked. A sharp spokesmen for the company pointed out that if there had indeed been a chemical leak from their plant, then their workers would have been the first ones affected. No such incident had taken place at the plant.

The next attack took place on September 13th at the home of Bertha Bench. Bench and her son, Orville, spotted the gasser and claimed it was a woman, dressed in man's clothing. Impressions from women's high-heeled shoes were discovered outside the window where the gas had been sprayed into the home.

This odd attack was the final incident involving the Mad Gasser of Mattoon. The case became famous as an example of supposed mass hysteria, with psychologists and skeptics touting the sensational nature of the reports and the infectious wave of reported attacks. None of these speculations really addressed the physical evidence or the countless witness sightings of an actual, physical gasser.

In present day Mattoon, most residents believe the mad gasser was actually a man by the name of Farley Llewellyn. Illinois historian and author, Scott Maruna, published his own work on the gasser in 2003. Maruna promotes the idea that the mentally ill Llewellyn was indeed the gasser. Maruna points out that many of the attacks were clustered around Llewellyn's home in Mattoon. He further believes Farley's sisters, Florence and Kathryn, had a hand in the attacks in an attempt to cover for their disturbed brother.

Farley Llewellyn attended the University of Illinois where he studied chemistry. By all accounts, the boy was a bit of a genius when it came to chemicals and had excelled at the subject in high school. Coming home from college however, he found that he was still an outsider, just as he had been in high school. Farley was rumored to be a homosexual, a very taboo lifestyle during the 1940s. He was also an alcoholic with personality and mental health issues. Farley's behavior grew very strange and people in town openly speculated that he was losing his mind. He built a laboratory at his home and kept it well stocked in order to continue his studies of chemistry.

Farley was arrested on September 10 and was sent to a state lunatic asylum where he spent the rest of his days. As noted above, the last of the Mattoon gas attacks happened just after Farley's arrest. Maruna speculates the last attack was carried out by one of Farley's sisters in an effort to take attention away from Farley's guilt in the gas attacks.

For some, this is the answer to the mystery in Mattoon. Others are still unsure. What about the attacks in Virginia ten years before? Were the two sprees connected? If it wasn't Farley, then who, or what, was the Mad Gasser? Most important of all, will he return again and, if so, what quiet little town will he terrorize?

The London Monster

London, England, 1789. An attractive young woman is out for an evening stroll when a large man begins to follow her. Nervous, she quickens her pace, hoping to reach friends nearby. The man continues to follow her; closer now, he begins to shout obscenities at the woman. In a sudden rush, he steps up behind her and stabs her in the buttocks with a needle. The woman cries out in pain and the man rushes off. He is long gone before anyone responds to the young woman's cries for help. She has become another victim of the dreaded London Monster.

Dubbed the London Monster, this strange criminal prowled the streets of London between the years of 1788 and 1790. His signature behavior was that of "piquerism" the pricking and/or stabbing of his victims with a needle, pin or even a knife. During his two-year spree, over fifty women fell victim to the attacks. Many were from wealthy families. They were often found with their clothing slashed and at times, bearing substantial wounds from the attack. Some women began to wear copper pans over their petticoats for protection from the attacker.

London residents were fearful of the attacker and angry that the police force seemed unable to capture him. Cries of incompetency led philanthropist John Julius Angerstein to offer a reward of one hundred pounds for the capture of the mad criminal. It wasn't just area women who were distraught. Innocent men began to worry about approaching women in the streets. Some even formed a "No Monster" club, wearing pins on their lapels to show women they were safe to approach.

In 1790, Anne Porter claimed she had seen the attacker and her companion, John Coleman had pursued the man. Coleman tracked the man down. It turned out to be a twenty-three year old, unemployed fellow by the name of Rhynwick Williams. Williams proclaimed his innocence but was arrested and charged with the crimes. Londoners, anxious for closure, made a mess of the initial trial. Cheers erupted in the courtroom when evidence was presented against Williams. Witnesses for the defense were booed and insulted. The affair became so absurd Williams was granted a retrial. The second trial was a bit more controlled. Some victim testimonies were contradictory and Williams had a firm alibi for at least one of the attacks. Still, he was found guilty and sentenced to a total of six years in prison. The attacks seemed to lessen during William's stint in jail, but there were still some reports of the London Monster, leading many to wonder if the real criminal had been captured.

Spring-heeled Jack

He had a frightening appearance — tall and thin, with the face of a devil; horrible and menacing. He could breathe out blue flames and his eyes looked like glowing balls of red fire. His hands had vicious metal talons with which he could rip clothing or flesh. He wore a large metal helmet and a tight fitting garment of white oilskin. Over this he wore a sweeping, black cloak. He was able to make amazing leaps crossing great distances, leaping over coaches, or from rooftop to rooftop. He was impossible to catch. He was known far and wide throughout London and the UK as Spring-heeled Jack.

Numerous reports of a strange attacker began to surface in 1837. The accounts continued to circulate through the year and into the next. Sir John Cowan, The Lord Mayor of London, received so many letters at the Mansion House that he talked about the subject at a public session held in January, 1838. While Cowan believed a lot of exaggeration was taking place, he had also received a report from a trusted associate leading him to believe something was definitely amiss. It seemed all of London was buzzing with tales of the creepy jumping villain. The Lord Mayor declared a vigilance committee was being formed to apprehend Spring-heeled Jack.

Historical records of the reports from 1837 are sketchy but they seem to fit the later patter of Spring-heeled Jack assaults. Some early reports claimed Jack disguised himself as a white bull or a white bear. Others promoted the idea Jack was actually some type of ghost or poltergeist out to stir up trouble. The attacks at this time were general assaults on women that included clothing being torn, and sometimes scratches and other surface wounds. Some of the attacks caused women to go into fits in the aftermath, with some claims that the victim never returned to her senses. These cases were usually investigated by the police with few answers being discovered. Officers were unsure exactly how to pursue Spring-heeled Jack.

While stories of Jack had circulated for some time, his real reign seemed to begin on the evening of February 20, 1838. Eighteen-year-old Jane Alsop heard a frantic ringing of the bell at the front gate of her family's home. It was almost nine o'clock, late for someone to be calling at the house in the little village of Old Ford on the outskirts of London. Going to the door, Jane saw a man standing in the dark and asked him why he was ringing so loudly. The figure responded that he was a policeman and said quickly:

"For God's sake, bring me a light, for we have caught Spring-heeled Jack here in the lane."

Jane rushed back in the house and retrieved a lit candle to carry to the officer. Back at the front door, Jane handed the light to the man. Instead of rushing off with the light however, he made a startling move. Throwing back his outer, long cloak, the man put the lit candle to his breast allowing the light to shine up and onto his hideous face. He spewed forth blue and white flames from his mouth, and his eyes lit up like red balls of fire. Jane saw that the man was wearing a large helmet and that below the cloak, he was attired in what looked like white oilskin. The man rushed towards her, grabbing her dress and the back of her neck. He managed to get her head and placed it under one of his arms, after which he proceeded to begin tearing her garments away. Jane saw his hands, which she reported were metallic claws. She screamed out for help and somehow managed to twist away from the attacker, running back towards the house. The attacker however, caught her as she reached the steps and began to tear at her neck and arms with his talons. Hearing the screams, Jane's older sister, Sarah Harrison, rushed from the house to aid her sister. Once the girls reached the safety of the house, family members threw open windows on the second floor and began to shout for the police. The weird figure disappeared back into the shadows.

Inside, Jane Alsop was in considerable shock. She was in pain from the various wounds inflicted on her by the attacker. Her dress was almost completely torn off and some of her hair had been pulled out. Police investigated the incident and suspects were picked up and questioned. Some officers seemed to believe the whole attack could be blamed on drunken behavior. Both Jane and her sister were quite sure the attacker was not drunk on the night in question. According to known public records, no one was ever brought to trial for the vicious assault on Jane Alsop.

Five days after the attack on Jane, Spring-heeled Jack surfaced in the East End of London. He approached a home at 2 Turner Street, an easy walk from the Alsop home. A servant boy answered the door and Jack threw open his cloak, revealing his terrible appearance. The boy screamed and Jack ran off.

On February 28, the attacker showed up in Limehouse in Green-dragon alley. Lucy Scales and her sister were walking when they were surprised by the assailant who temporarily blinded Lucy with a bright flash of blue flame. Lucy fell to the ground and went into fits. Oddly, the attacker simply walked away from the scene without further assaulting the girls. It seemed he was satisfied with the chaos he had caused. The description Lucy gave police fit the profile received from Jane Alsop. Lucy added that she saw the man carrying a small lantern or lamp, similar to those used by the police.

With the sensational stories of Jack circulating, imitators appeared left and right. Most were arrested quickly and didn't fit the correct profile of what was believed to be the real Spring-heeled Jack's attacks. In the following years, Jack supposedly made appearances in various locations from the sprawl of London, to the Midlands of Scotland. Few convincing reports have been dug up from the archives, but Spring-heeled Jack was far from finished.

A series of incidents broke out in Peckham in 1872 and another flap in Sheffield in 1873. Both cases involved a tall man in white accosting people and causing fright. Later, historians digging into the legend of Spring-heeled Jack often tie these incidents into the mythos, but it is important to note neither of these attacks really seemed to be the same figure, but rather men attempting to imitate ghosts in order to frighten people.

The British Army camp at Aldershot became the next stage for Spring-heeled Jack to play on. The year was 1877 and the incidents were reported in the military newspaper, *"Sheldrake's Aldershot & Sandhurst Military Gazette."* According to the paper:

"Someone or other appears to have made up his mind to play some rather questionable pranks with the sentries at this Camp while on night duty. About a week ago it appears, but we do not vouch for the correctness of the story, a sentry was on duty at the North camp, and about midnight someone came towards him, who refused to answer to the usual challenge of 'who comes there', and after dodging about the sentry box in a fantastic fashion for some little time, made off with astonishing swiftness, not however until the sentry had loaded his rifle and fired, but without any effect. 'Spring-heeled Jack', as he has been termed, in Camp, then paid a similar visit to the sentry on duty near the cemetery, who also fired, but alas without hitting the object at which he aimed. What or who the individual who is thus amusing himself might be we do not know, but such little bits of fun might be carried just too far; and enjoyment of this kind had better be discontinued before one of the nocturnal pranks leads to unpleasant results."

About a month later, the same paper reported Spring-heeled Jack had told someone his goal was to "frighten the British army." Purportedly Jack managed to slap one sentry a number of times, wrestle with another, and avoid several pursuers with great bounds across the common.

The Illustrated Police News reports Jack disappeared for a brief time then resurfaced towards the end of summer. He once again haunted the military camp, harassing sentries and repeating some of his same antics. One incident near the powder magazine in the North camp is notable, according to the *News*:

"Here, having nearly frightened the sentry out of his wits, by slapping his face with his death-like hand, he disappeared, hopping and bounding in to the mist."

Later that year, the *News* reported again on Spring-heeled Jack, this time placing him in the Newport area. If we are to believe the report, this time Jack changed his normal attire in favor of animal skins. According to the story, the neighborhood had:

"...been disturbed each night by a man dressed in a sheep skin, or something of the kind, with a long white tail to it. The man who is playing this mischief has springs to his boots, and can jump to a height of 15 or 20 feet. The other night he jumped upon a college, and got into a window on the roof, and so frightened the ladies that one has not yet recovered from the shock. Some other people were so much frightened by this object, that every night a large mob of men, armed with sticks and stones, assemble and attempt to catch him, but to no avail."

The report also claims that shots were fired on Jack but he either dodged the bullets, or they had no effect on him; possibly because of the hide he was wearing. While the report is fascinating, later historians have some doubt as to its authenticity, due to the *Police News'* reputation for sensationalizing stories, and according to some people, outright fabricating them.

There are other listings of purported sightings of Spring-heeled Jack in the following years. Some assert he was in Manchester and Liverpool in the late 1880s. What appears to have been his last appearance occurred in Liverpool at the end of September, 1904. An article published about Jack years later in 1967 by the *"Liverpool Daily Post"* has this to say about the 1904 account:

"In September, 1904, the Springing Terror made his last appearance, this time in William Henry Street, when hundreds of local folk watched in awe as the pathetic creature leaped up and down the length of Everton Street. After more than ten minutes of leaps which would embarrass present day Olympic high jumpers (and pole vaulters too) he was seen to jump clean over the terraced houses from Stitt Street to Haigh Street, and then hop back across the slate roofs to Salisbury Street, after which he was never seen again."

Some stories at the time suggested Jack wore boots with springs on the heels or perhaps, "India-rubber sole boots" that aided him in making his fantastic leaps. While a fanciful idea, neither of these types of shoes would have allowed him to make the jumps he was purported to make, nor were they practical in use.

Supernatural elements have been frequently introduced to explain how Jack was able to accomplish his feats. These theories include speculation Spring-heeled Jack wasn't human at all, but actually an alien and represents early human-alien contact. This particular theory was primarily generated as a result of an article by J. Vyner in the March/April 1961 issue of *"Flying Saucer Review."* In the article titled "The Mystery of Springheel Jack", Vyner speculated that Jack was part of an alien aircrew that had to bail out over England and that he was merely searching for a way home.

Writer Peter Haining authored the only full-length book to address the topic of Spring-heeled Jack. In *"The Legend and Bizarre Crimes of Spring-Heeled Jack,"* Haining promotes the theory that Jack was in reality Henry, Marquis of Waterford. Henry was a wild young man, prone to excessive drinking and fighting. There's little evidence however, to support the idea he was actually the spring-heeled villain.

Other writers have suggested Jack was a practitioner of some dark, occult art from which he derived his strange abilities. Some have even proposed Jack was some kind of demonic entity, summoned to our world to wreak havoc. Whatever his true origins, Jack's bizarre behaviors made him a prime subject for storytellers, and he was featured in plays and Penny Dreadful stories throughout the late 1800s. Spring-heeled Jack holds a strong and firm part in English legend and folklore.

Chapter Five
Grinning Men, Reptoids and Cold Characters

The Carolina Grinning Man

I've seen the Grinning Man.

It almost sounds like a silly statement, bringing to mind the image of a man with a large grin, perhaps a bit goofy, and certainly not malevolent. But sometimes it's the most subtle things that are the creepiest.

You see, the version of the grinning man I saw was not some fellow with a simple, silly smile on his face. No, this was a very strange character, certainly out of place and somehow quite, quite disturbing.

The encounter occurred in the 1980s in a rural part of North Carolina. I was in the passenger seat of a car being driven by a friend, Tom. I'd known Tom for a number of years and we frequently took trips and explored back roads around the area. Tom often stated he believed I was a magnet for weird events and that he took a chance hanging out with me so much. His assertions were proven late one afternoon as we drove along a winding road lined with trees on both sides. There was only an occasional farm along this route and it was a pleasant drive. We cruised along at a fairly moderate pace, maybe forty-five miles an hour, not really in any hurry. As we rounded one curve, the road headed into a long curve in the opposite direction. Looking ahead, I saw someone standing on the right side of the road just ahead. I focused on the figure, thinking something looked a bit odd, and as we got closer I realized the man was wearing a long coat and hat. It was late summer and even the evenings were warm that time of year. Why was this man wearing a coat? I motioned to Tom and asked him if he saw the man. He shook his head in an affirmative reply, transfixed on the figure. The car seemed to slow down as we approached the stranger. I wasn't sure if Tom was actually letting off on the gas or if something else was happening. Later he would have no clear memory as to whether or not he was lifting his foot from the gas pedal or if something else caused the slow-motion effect.

As the car approached the figure, he came clearly into focus. He was wearing a long, old-fashioned coat and a formal hat. The hat was cut like a top hat but didn't seem quite as tall. His right hand was gloved and he held it up, just under his chin. It looked as if he was rubbing his thumb and fingers together. His left arm hung down behind his back. The entire ensemble looked rather Victorian, except visible under the coat was a large shiny belt. The oddest thing however, was his expression.

He was grinning.

A wide, leering grin. Impossibly large. It distorted his face and reminded me in that moment of the Joker, the Batman's crazed villain always depicted with a grinning face. Everything seemed to move in slow motion as we drifted past the strange, tall man. His gaze followed us as we rolled by him. We almost came to a complete stop. I felt a chill as if we had just crossed over the path of something wholly unnatural. I turned around, peering through the back window to get another look at the figure. He was there, standing in the road now, looking towards our car but as quick as I had turned around, I hadn't seen him move to his new position. It seemed impossible and added to the creepiness of the whole affair.

I turned to Tom who was looking in the rearview mirror, white as a sheet and eyes wide in disbelief. Turning back, I saw the grinning figure still standing in the road, staring at us with his hideous smile. I watched for a moment, then we rounded another curve and I lost sight of him.

The car seemed to speed up quickly and I thought that Tom had slammed the gas pedal down. I immediately asked him to stop and go back. He, of course, expressed the opinion that I was crazy and there was no way he was stopping let alone going back to the spot where the crazy guy was standing.

"He's probably some psycho who watched Friday the 13th too many times!" Tom asserted.

I didn't think that was the case. We were in an area with few houses and we hadn't seen any other vehicles parked along the road, not that there was any place to really pull over anyway.

"Tom, there was something unnatural about that character. I want to get another look at him."

"You're damn right he was unnatural; he's some psycho!"

The debate raged for a couple of miles before I could convince Tom to turn around and at least go back to the bend in the road.

"We'll go just around the bend and see if he's still standing in the road, or if he's waiting for another car to come," I plead.

Tom reluctantly agreed to the plan and we made a U-turn in the road heading back to the location we'd last seen the grinning man. Rounding the bend slowly, we scanned the road ahead. There was nothing there. Tom completely stopped the car in the middle of the road and just sat there within sight of the spot where we had seen the figure. I jumped out of the car to Tom's loud protests, and ran up to the spot where the figure had stood. I was more curious than concerned and I was confident that Tom would not leave me stranded, despite his aggravation over my actions.

I searched the area where the grinning figure had stood. There was no sign of a vehicle anywhere, nowhere someone could have pulled off and parked, no hidden driveways. There was in fact, very little room on the side of the road in this location. There was a deep ditch very close to the road and the tree line started directly on the other side of the ditch. There was room for someone to stand here and there and I found the spot where we had seen the figure. There weren't any visible footprints but the heavy grass did look as though someone had recently stood in it.

The one odd thing in the area was a strange smell. It was electrical in nature, as though a transformer or something like it had been burning. There were no power lines here, however, and I couldn't find anything to explain the odor. Tom had pulled the car up, yelling out the window and insisting he would leave me there if I didn't get back in the car so we could leave. I complied after a moment, glancing once more up and down in each direction in one last search for the odd, grinning man. There was nothing.

As soon as I climbed in the car, Tom made another quick U-turn and we sped off. In my friend's mind, the entire incident simply reaffirmed his belief strange things happened whenever he spent too much time around me. I was left wondering about what exactly we had seen. Clearly, someone had stood in the grass where we had seen the grinning figure, yet there was no route the man could have taken to get away from the area quickly. I vowed to return to the area myself and investigate further. I also resolved to myself I would have to start hanging out with people who were just as curious about the unknown as I was!

Later that night, a couple of odd events added to the mystery of the day. Just before nine o'clock, flashes of lightning began to fill the sky, clearly a storm was moving in. About an hour later, Tom called to tell me the house next door to his got struck by lightning and had caught fire. Tom was actually outside getting his dog in out of the weather when it happened.

"Sparks shot up everywhere," he reported. The roof of the house started burning. Fortunately no one was injured and the fire department was able to get the flames out before extensive damage was done. It was an unusual event and I was immediately reminded of the electrical, burning smell that had been in the area around the grinning man. Was he an omen of the event that occurred that night? Some may consider such things mere coincidence, but synchronicities like these often fall into place in the aftermath of encounters with paranormal figures.

The night got even more interesting when, a half hour after Tom's call, another friend rang me to report his sister and mother had just sighted a UFO. The family lived about five miles from Tom, and I learned the sighting had taken place about the same time Tom witnessed the lightning strike on his neighbor's home.

At this point, the rain was fairly heavy, but despite the nasty weather, I drove to the location on the off chance something else would happen. Sadly, there were no other anomalous incidents in the area that night. Asking around the next day, I discovered another couple had witnessed strange lights in the sky the previous night. All four people who sighted the UFO reported the same thing — a bright light low in the sky that shimmered and pulsed. Initially, the light was white and changed color to amber, then to blue-white and then back to white.

On a number of occasions, I returned to the location where Tom and I had seen the grinning man. My propensity to investigate strange sightings and events was fueled by my desire to decipher what had happened. The closest house to the spot of the sighting was several miles away. Carefully, I asked around the area, trying to root out other sightings or strange events — not always an easy task in the country.

Obviously, I couldn't try knocking at the door of a random farmhouse to ask if they'd seen any strange characters about!

The riddle remained. Who was the grinning man? Why did he appear and where did he go? There's never been an answer that completely satisfied the mystery for me. There was scant information available on grinning men at the time. I read again John Keel's accounts as well as the few other related things I could find. Opinions as to the figure's origin were divided, many thought he was some type of alien, some believed he was a cryptid or perhaps a ghost. The most amusing input I received came from a contactee who assured me the grinning man was simply a 'friendly space brother.' Great opinion, but friendliness was the last thing that radiated from the chap that I saw on that lonely back road.

The New Jersey Grinning Man

A UFO of blazing white light the size of a car was reported by several people on the night of October 11, 1966. The craft was first seen outside of Pompton, New Jersey near a large DuPont explosives factory. A police officer and his wife observed the craft as it moved north over the hills. Once over the hills, the craft was spotted again, this time by two law enforcement officers on patrol, Sergeant Benjamin Thompson and Patrolman Edward Wester of the Wanaque Reservoir Police. The two officers watched the UFO drop over the reservoir, Thompson claiming the light emanating from it was so bright he was blinded for twenty minutes after witnessing it.

At the same time, forty miles to the south, another strange encounter was unfolding. In the town of Elizabeth, New Jersey, two boys were walking home along Fourth and New Jersey Streets. The boys, James Yanchitis and Martin "Mouse" Munov, reached a corner parallel to the New Jersey Turnpike. At this location, the turnpike is elevated with a steep drop down to Fourth Street. A high, wire fence serves as a barricade between the street and the turnpike. At this well-lit location, the two boys witnessed a very odd character standing behind the fence. Yanchitis, who saw the figure first, later commented, "I don't know how he got there. He was the biggest man I ever saw."

Yanchitis caught the attention of his friend, Mouse, and pointed to the tall man. According to "Mouse" Munov, "I looked around and there he was behind that fence, just standing there. He pivoted around and looked right at us...and then he grinned a big old grin."

John Keel went to Elizabeth, NJ to interview the boys. UFO researcher James Moseley and actor Chuck McCann, a UFO enthusiast, went with him. The boys were interviewed separately and both told the same story. They claimed the man they had seen was over six feet tall. He was wearing a green coverall that sparkled and shimmered, reflecting the streetlights. At his waist was a wide black belt. McCann, who was present for the interviews, was used as a reference point since he was 6' 2" tall. Both boys asserted the grinning man was not only taller than McCann, but also broader. The grinning man, they said, had a dark complexion and beady, little, round eyes. Oddly, neither of the boys could remember any other features on the man's face, nor could they remember any hair. The boys didn't notice the man's hands, and his feet were obscured by underbrush.

The boys did not linger in the area after seeing the man. There had been some violent attacks in the neighborhood so they weren't taking chances. Keel heard rumors that a "tall green man" had chased a couple down Fourth Street that night. He was unable to substantiate the tale.

John Keel considered various possibilities to explain the presence of the strange man, but nothing seemed to add up. On the surface, it was merely a tall man with a big grin, but why was he standing behind the fence near the turnpike? Yanchitis and Munoz believed the man was staring at a house across the street. Was it mere coincidence the man turned up at the same time a UFO flap had occurred?

Indrid Cold

Over the years, Keel would hear stories of this creepy, grinning man on a number of occasions, but the most famous of the lot appeared no less than a month later.

November 2, 1966. On Interstate 77 between Marietta, Ohio and Mineral Wells, West Virginia, a sewing machine salesman named Woodrow Derenberger had a strange encounter. Derenberger was driving through the rain on his way home to Mineral Wells when a strange object came up from behind him. At first, he thought it was simply a car speeding up to pass his slower-moving truck. When the object was in front of him however, it turned sideways on the highway and began to slow down, forcing Derenberger to stop and pull off the road to avoid hitting it. According to reports, Derenberger said the object was "shaped like the chimney of a kerosene lamp".

A six-foot man with a dark complexion and elongated eyes emerged from the weird object and approached Derenberger. The man wore a dark coat and shiny, blue pants. He approached Derenberger's truck sporting a huge grin. The stranger proceeded to have a conversation with Derenberger telepathically.

The conversation consisted of fairly simple questions. During the course of it, the man told Derenberger his name was "Cold" and he was from a country "less powerful" than the United States. The grinning man told Derenberger he would return and climbed into his strange craft. The ship then departed, moving straight up with only a slight noise.

The episode changed Derenberger's life. By December of 1967, he had divorced his wife, moved to another state and married a younger woman. He had become a "contactee," famous in UFO circles for having repeated encounters with the strange man called "Indrid Cold." Derenberger claimed that Cold, along with others, visited him at his farm. They would often arrive in automobiles and have long talks with the former salesman. Unidentified lights and objects were seen by many witnesses in the skies over Derenberger's home.

Derenberger, or "Woody" as he became fondly known, openly talked about his encounters, appearing on radio and television and working with UFO organizations. His initial report was picked up by UPI and circulated around the world. He would later report that "Indrid Cold" claimed to be from a planet called "Lanulos" in "the galaxy of Genemedes." Woody also claimed to have visited Cold's planet and saw exotic plants and animals. The people, he said, sometimes wore colorful clothing, but often remained completely nude.

Two weeks after Derenberger released the details of his encounter, a pair of strangers showed up in Mineral Wells, West Virginia. The duo went from door to door telling various stories to explain who they were. At different times, they claimed to be salesmen, sometimes of hardware, sometimes selling Bibles. They told some residents they were Mormon missionaries from Salem, Oregon.

While accounts of the so-called "Men in Black" have been common around UFO flaps, this particular pair really stood out. One of the men was described as being short with dark hair. His complexion was said to be olive-toned like those of the Mediterranean region. His companion was the opposite. Tall, with blond hair and a light complexion fitting the typical "Nordic" body type often associated with UFO accounts of the period. While the men claimed to be salesmen and missionaries, they were quite fixated on Derenberger and his encounter. At each stop, they barraged homeowners with questions. They wanted people's opinions about Woody Derenberger, the encounter he'd had and what they thought about Indrid Cold.

In yet another strange synchronicity, Keel reports in *"The Mothman Prophecies"* that while the two supposed missionaries from Salem were in Mineral Wells grilling residents about Derenberger, there was a UFO flap over Salem!

Derenberger dictated his contactee experiences to Ohio UFO investigator Harold W. Hubbard and the two published a book, *"Visitors from Lanulos"* in 1971. The book is rather typical of contactee literature of the period, with tales of saucer rides to other planets and exotic humanoid-type aliens with benevolent attitudes.

Keel wrote the foreword for the book and is careful about how he introduces the work, stating:

"I cannot endorse his story but I do feel I know the man well enough to give him a character reference. The important thing is that he seems to be telling the truth as he knows it. He sincerely believes that these things happened to him." Keel further states: "I have talked to 'contactee' claimants who are doctors, lawyers, newspapermen, police officers and pilots. Woody has a lot of company—sane, reputable people. Perhaps we are the ones who have been insane for ignoring them for so long. Strange, unbelievable things are now happening to people all over the world. By listening to the handful of courageous ones, like Woodrow Derenberger, we may at last gain some real insight into what is really behind the UFO phenomenon. I'm not asking you to believe any of it. But I am asking you to listen to what he has to say. Incredible though it may seem, it is very possible that these very same things could happen to you tomorrow."

It seems clear Indrid Cold and the "Grinning Man" are two very different entities. Forever tied together however, through the work of John Keel. The lines were blurred even further with 2002's film version of "The Mothman Prophecies" starring Richard Gere. The film was loosely based on Keel's book of the same name. Like most Hollywood versions of books, many liberties were taken with the story and characters. Indrid Cold became a figure who spoke telepathically, yet also made cryptic phone calls. For entertainment value, it's a good film but I always encourage people to read the book since so much was missing from the big screen story.

More Grinning Men

John Keel also spoke with the Lilly family in Point Pleasant, West Virginia about a grinning man. In meeting with the Lillys, Keel discovered that Linda, a young female member of the family, had seen a strange figure in her bedroom at night. Based on the report, Keel classified this character as a grinning man. According to Linda, she woke up one night and found a large figure standing over her bed:

"It was a man, a big man. Very broad. I couldn't see his face very well but I could see that he was grinning at me."

The young girl screamed out for her mother but the grinning man merely walked to the side of the bed and stood over the girl. Panicked, she hid under the covers and screamed once again for help. When she managed to peek out from the blankets, she found the weird man had disappeared. Linda's mother reached the room to find her daughter very shaken. She tried to convince the girl it was simply a nightmare but the young woman insisted she saw a real, physical man in the room. "There is a man in my room! There is!" No amount of discussion could change the girl's opinion about what she had experienced. After the incident, she refused to sleep alone. When pressed by Keel and his associates for more details about the man, Linda reported he was wearing a "checkered shirt."

During his years of investigation, Keel found other accounts of so-called grinning men. In 1968, framers in New York's Delaware County chased a giant, broad-shouldered grinning man with an unruly shock of silver hair. They reported that the figure was over six feet tall and when they chased him, he displayed remarkable agility, making incredible leaps across wide ditches. The figure proved impossible to catch. Some of the witnesses who claimed to have had face-to-face confrontations with the man stated he had small eyes and a wide, fixed grin.

A similar figure plagued people in Provincetown, Massachusetts between 1966 and 1967. Like the Delaware grinning man, he was never apprehended.

Years after my own encounter, I was able to discuss grinning men with John Keel. I related my account to him and he listened, fascinated, but not surprised. He told me he still received accounts of grinning men and he believed there was a definite connection to UFOs, since there were so many cases of the two showing up in the same time frame. He advised me to correlate UFO sightings and related events to the period when I saw the grinning figure. I told him about the strange lightning strike, and the UFO sighting reported to me that night. I had already searched for other sightings in the area and only managed to find one other that same week. It was a very rural area however, and such things may not very likely to have been reported.

Interesting enough, after the discussion with Keel, I decided to expand the area of my search and take another look at unusual events during the time of my encounter. I contacted a small UFO group I was familiar with in the next state over and found they had recorded several sightings in the time frame I was examining. Even stranger, they had record someone had reported a so-called 'phantom clown' the same week I had seen the grinning man. The woman who had sent the account said she was driving home one evening down a country lane. Rounding a bend in the lane, she was startled to see a figure standing in the road. He wore a long tattered coat, a large hat and had a strange grin on his face. She claimed he had bright clothing on beneath the coat, and she thought he looked like a 'hobo clown.' Unfortunately, the report was brief and I was unable to locate the woman to obtain further details.

Due to my own encounter with a grinning man, I've always been especially interested in accounts of the figure. In the late 1990s, an associate approached me about his encounter with a weird grinning figure that damaged his work truck. Jonathan was working for a moving company in Virginia when he had his encounter, related here in his own words:

"We were moving an entire office building from Richmond, Virginia to Norfolk, Virginia. It was a big job and because our company was experiencing a very busy period, we only had one truck for this move. We also had a short time to get the whole job done. We got an early start, had the truck fully loaded and made it to Norfolk by late afternoon. We still had to unload and get back to Richmond to load the truck a second time that night. The new office building was much larger than the one the company was moving from and it had a big loading dock, which made our offload much easier. We had grabbed lunch on the way to Norfolk, so by the time we got there, we started the offload right away. About an hour into it, the other guy and I were both moving small items that took only one of us. We were in a rhythm where he would be in the building and I would be on the truck and we'd pass in the hallway. I was just going into the back of the truck when out of the corner of my eye I noticed someone standing down by the truck.

I stepped over to the edge of the dock to see who it was. Weirdest guy I've ever seen in my life. He had on a bright green, long-sleeve top. It was sort of a lime green and I thought, wow, how ugly that thing is. He was also wearing a big, silver belt and dark pants. It was like a bad Rock and Roll outfit or something. Over all of this, he had on a raincoat, kind of shabby looking. I didn't know if he was a homeless guy, somebody on drugs or what. The creepy thing was his smile. It just didn't seem natural because it was so big. It's like that old thing about grinning ear to ear, this kid really was! Nobody's mouth looks like that, not if they're normal anyway. I asked him what he wanted but all he did was smile at me like his face was frozen. He didn't budge an inch. I had a funny feeling in the pit of my stomach. Just then, my partner called out from behind me and asked if I was slacking off. I turned and replied that no, I was trying to run this weird guy off.

"What guy?" he asked.

I looked back around and the smiling man was gone. Just then, we both heard what sounded like someone knocking on the hood of the truck. We jumped down and went to the front of the truck, but no one was there and there wasn't any sign of anything wrong. We kind of shook it off and got back to work. After we had everything unloaded, we climbed in the truck, ready to head back to Richmond. The truck wouldn't start though. In fact, it had no power at all. It seemed that the battery was dead. We ended up having to wait around until the company could get a mechanic over to look at the truck. They had to tow the truck to a repair center and we found out that the whole electrical system was fried. I didn't tell anybody at work about the weird smiling guy, but I'm convinced that it was him knocking on the truck and that he did something to the electrical system."

Neither Jonathan, nor his partner reported having seen a UFO or any other strange phenomenon. However, digging around, I uncovered a number of UFO reports from the weeks before and after the men encountered the destructive grinning man.

Reptoids...Italian Style

On the cold night of December 6th, 1978, twenty-six-year old Pier Fortunato Zanfretta had the first in a series of bizarre encounters with otherworldly creatures. Zanfretta was employed as a private security guard and was on patrol in the small Italian village of Torriglia. Traveling carefully on the icy roads, Zanfretta was on his way to check on the empty home of Dr. Ettore Righi when his car suddenly died. The Fiat's engine, lights and radio all went off at the same moment not far from the Righi home. Zanfretta spotted four lights moving around the garden of the home and believed thieves were attempting to break into the house. Revolver and flashlight in hand, Zanfretta slipped into the home's open gate and followed a rock wall toward the lights, hoping to surprise the would-be thieves. It was Zanfretta however, who received the surprise.

Preparing to leap out at the criminals, the young guard felt something touch his shoulder from behind. Whirling around, he was confronted, not by a human thief, but by a frightening creature that he later described as:

"An enormous green, ugly and frightful creature, with undulating skin...as though he were very fat or dressed in a loose, gray tunic...no less than ten feet tall." Zanfretta later stated the creature had "greenish skin" and "yellow, triangular eyes and red veins across the forehead". The creature also had points on the sides of its face. Many in UFO circles believe this was an example of what has come to be called a "reptilian" or "reptoid."

After rushing away from the weird creature before him, Zanfretta reached his car only to see a bright light rise up behind him. Looking over his shoulder, he observed a massive, flat, triangular-shaped craft emitting a blinding light. The craft was bigger than the house that it was rising over. A blast of heat rolled over the guard as he struggled to the radio in his car. At 12:15, he reached the security company's radio operator, Carlo Toccalino. Toccalino listened to Zanfretta, but at first he couldn't understand the incoherent ramblings coming from the guard. It was clear Zanfretta was very excited, the operator heard him repeating, "My God, are they ugly!". He asked the guard to calm down and describe the men who had assaulted him at which point Zanfretta replied, "No, they aren't men, they aren't men." Then suddenly, the communication ended.

The company's security chief promptly sent another patrol car to the location. Foul weather and dangerous driving conditions made it difficult to reach the site and an hour had passed before the second car arrived. The guards, Walter Lauria and Raimondo Mascia arrived at 1:15. They found Zanfretta lying in a prone position in front of the house. Seeing the two men walking towards him, Zanfretta leapt up and pointed his revolver at them. Seeing his panicked state, the two guards rushed Zanfretta before he could harm them, or himself. The two men later stated that, despite the fact he had been lying on the frozen ground, Zanfretta was warm.

The Carabinieri (Italian Police) were called to the scene to investigate. They found strange marks on the ground behind the house. It was clear something large and heavy had left the two impressions. The marks were nine feet in diameter and shaped like horseshoes. Some speculated they were landing marks from a UFO. During the investigation, fifty-two residents of the village reported seeing bright lights emanating from the direction of the Righi house that night.

Reporters got wind of the story and the press had a field day, many making fun of it, at least those who would cover a UFO story. Some simply reported the incident as it was recounted; others were more brutal calling Zanfretta everything from a mental case to an outright liar. However, one reporter took the incident seriously. Rino Di Stefano was working for *"Il Corriere Mercantile"* the local Genoa daily newspaper. Di Stefano found the case intriguing and wrote several articles chronicling the events. Not only were there fifty-two other witnesses to the UFO's lights, the reporter also found it unlikely that Zanfretta, a father of two and a reputed "honest man" would make up such a story. As Di Stefano wrote:

"Zanfretta didn't want to be famous. He refused the notoriety because he was worried about his job and his family."

Trying to understand what he had gone through and uncover more of the facts, Zanfretta agreed to undergo hypnosis. Dr. Mauro Moretti, a psychotherapist and member of the Italian Association of Medical Hypnosis conducted the sessions. Under hypnosis, Zanfretta recalled more details of his weird experience learning that, not only had he encountered aliens, they had also abducted him.

Further details emerged from Zanfretta while under hypnosis. He said the creatures didn't speak to him in Italian, but used a "luminous device" to translate their own language. Disturbingly, Zanfretta also said the creatures, from a planet in the "third galaxy," "...want to talk with us and that they will soon return in large numbers."

The saga of Pier Zanfretta doesn't end there, though. He had yet another encounter with aliens on the evening of December 26th. On a rain-soaked road near the Scoffera Pass, the guard lost control of his car, not due to the slick pavement, but due to "something" taking over the controls. A panicked call on his radio once again sent assistance his way, but not before he radioed back reporting, "The car has stopped. I saw a bright light. Now I am getting out."

An hour later, Zanfretta was found in a nearby field by officers who had answered the call. Despite the pouring rain, Zanfretta was warm and dry.

The Carabinieri found themselves again investigating a scene involving this lone security guard. Zanfretta's Smith & Wesson revolver was recovered and five bullets had been fired. The guard claimed he had no recollection of using the weapon. When the Carabinieri examined Zanfretta's car, they noted it was "hot as an oven" inside and out, despite the cold rain. Even more puzzling, the car was surrounded by shoe prints that measured twenty inches long by eight inches wide. A bare spot was obvious between the sole and heel of the prints, but no one could offer any explanation for the tracks. Since shots had been fired at the scene, the Carabinieri launched a probe into the incident and issued an official report. The data was collected on January 3, 1979. It seemed no one really knew what to do with the information. A year later, January 11, 1980, the papers were rubber stamped "no crime committed" and filed away.

While the Carabinieri were reviewing the case file, they informed both the Italian Department of the Interior and other military commands. They rated the reliability of Zanfretta's weird accounts as good. In 1978, Italy was having a massive wave of UFO sightings, interest was at a high point and the military and government were both paying attention.

Zanfretta became a bit of a celebrity but he still didn't like the attention that was focused on him. He agreed to another hypnosis session, this time allowing it to be televised in an attempt to show he was not a mental case. In a trance state, Zanfretta related his bizarre tale of an alien encounter and abduction. Viewer numbers were in the hundreds of thousands, but the show didn't have the effect Zanfretta was hoping for. Skeptics merely used the show to add fuel to their fire, and it took a long while for the attention to finally die off.

Zanfretta was examined by a prominent neurologist from Genoa who pronounced him "perfectly sane" but in a "state of shock". The attention on the security guard had grown well beyond the borders of Italy, with stories of his experiences appearing in media around the world. It was months before attention on the case started to die down.

But yet again, Zanfretta's tale was not finished.

The guard was abducted again on the night of July 30, 1979. This time he was riding a motorcycle in a residential neighborhood in Genoa. Again, he was found by fellow security officers, this time at the top of Mount Fasce. After this abduction, Zanfretta had another hypnosis session. At his own request, Zanfretta was injected with a truth serum prior to the session. Under these conditions, the guard affirmed all of the previous information he had given about his abductions was true and that during the last encounter he had been taken to a spaceship by a "green light." Professor Marco Marchesan, who injected the man with the truth serum stated:

"No human being can knowingly lie while he is under Pentothal treatment, so I think it's very probable Zanfretta had these encounters."

A few months later, December 2, 1979, Zanfretta was taken again. Other officers on patrol reported spotting a UFO and one even fired his revolver at it to no avail. As if Zanfretta's encounters couldn't get any stranger, the details that emerged from this latest incident introduced a new element.

A Grinning Man.

Stopping at a self-service gas station in Genoa, Zanfretta climbed out of his patrol car only to hear someone calling for him. In the shadows outside of the station was a strange figure. According to Zanfretta, the man was a tall, human looking figure with a bald, egg-shaped head. He was dressed in a checkered suit and wore what appeared to be a steel breastplate instead of a shirt. The grinning man's voice compelled Zanfretta to do as he was told. He was commanded to drive his car into a cloud hovering just above the ground nearby. Once inside the cloud, the entire car was lifted and transported into a spaceship.

During one of his last abductions, the aliens gave Zanfretta a mysterious object. It was a large, transparent sphere with a pyramid inside. Sparks discharged and jumped from the vertices of the pyramid towards the inside of the sphere. The beings told Zanfretta that, with the sphere, it was possible to understand them and how they lived. During a hypnosis session, Zanfretta recounted that he didn't want to take the sphere. He told the aliens he was finished and wanted nothing to do with them or the sphere. They were insistent however, and told Zanfretta he was to give the sphere to a man named Dr. J. Allen Hynek. Zanfretta claimed to have no idea who Hynek was. Hynek was best known for his UFO research and his part in the US government's Project Blue Book, an attempt to discredit UFO sightings. Pressed further about the mysterious sphere and pyramid, Zanfretta stated he hid the object in the hills outside Genoa and that he is waiting. Hynek passed away in 1986, so if the sphere was truly supposed to go to him the opportunity has been lost.

Zanfretta was abducted two more times-once in February of 1980 and later the same year in August. His last hypnosis sessions took another weird turn when he began to speak in what was believed to be an alien language a portion of the time. He was out of control and would not cooperate with Dr. Moretti, who was conducting the session. One of the last things he communicated in English was:

"To believe or not to believe doesn't mean anything. Each thing in its own time."

Journalist Rino Di Stefano stayed in contact with Zanfretta over the years, eventually writing a book about the case. *"IL Caso Zanfretta"* was published in 1984. It remains the only chronicle that details this amazing case.

Abducted by Crocodile Men

A strange alien abduction case surfaced in Calgary, in the province of Alberta, Canada in 1967. The case involved a young man named David Seewaldt and his encounter with a flying saucer piloted by crocodile-skinned aliens.

David Seewaldt was fourteen years old at the time of the incident. It was November 17, 1967. After a day of high school, David went to a friend's house a few blocks away from his own family home. David and his friend Matt had a routine of lifting weights on a regular basis, an attempt to emulate the pro wrestlers they watched each week on television. David knew his parents didn't come home until five thirty each evening, so it gave him and his friend over an hour to lift weights. On this particular day, the boys finished their routines around five forty-five. David put his coat on, said farewell to his friend and headed out to walk home. It was cold outside since the weather had started changing. The walk was normally a short one to his home and, this evening, David decided to take a shortcut. He took off across a field when suddenly, he heard a humming sound. At first, he thought perhaps it was a swarm of bees. He looked around and found nothing, then suddenly in the sky above him he saw a large, silver, disc-shaped craft. On its upper dome were flashing, colored lights. The ship moved quickly through the sky, then turned and started to swoop down towards him. The craft, it was later learned, was as large as a house and hovered thirty to forty feet above the ground.

At around six thirty, David rushed into his house. He almost ran into his older sister, Angela, as he darted up the stairs and into his bedroom.

"What's the matter with you stupid? You're late!" she shouted after him. Angela followed David up the stairs to his bedroom. When she got to the door, she found her brother crouching on the floor, trying to hide under his bed. He was in a panic and clearly afraid of something. Angela noticed David was only wearing one shoe. Nervously, the boy peered out the window.

"What's wrong? Did you drop a barbell on your head?" David didn't get the joke. All he could manage was a stuttered question.

"Is...is it gone?"

"Is what gone?" Angela replied.

"The flying saucer! It chased me across the field from Matt's house!" It was as if the statement didn't really register with Angela.

"You're acting much weirder than you usually do. Why are you so late?"

"It followed me," David responded. "It came toward me, and then...and then...I don't remember. I was coming in the door!" Angela asked David why he had stayed at Matt's house so long that night.

"But I left there at a quarter to six like I usually do," he answered. David told his sister about the flying saucer he had seen in the field and how it swept down towards him, causing him to run the rest of the way home. When Angela pointed out that he still should have been home in mere minutes after leaving his friend's house, David could not understand where the missing time had gone or why he couldn't remember anything else. Somehow, he had lost half an hour.

As to David's missing shoe, it was later discovered outside, along the road. Likely, he had lost it in his frantic run to get to the safety of his house. Angela realized her brother had experienced something strange and she pushed him to tell their parents about the sighting. The Seewaldts were unsure about how to handle the situation. They knew their son was not prone to making up stories or telling lies, but this was well outside of the norm.

David's sighting of the flying saucer and his loss of time proved to be just the tip of the iceberg.

In the days following his encounter David changed. Normally, he was a calm young man, good-natured and easygoing. Suddenly, he became very nervous. He was constantly looking about as if he was being followed. He jumped at sudden noises, movements in his direction made him uneasy. Additionally, he experienced dizziness and disorientation. The Seewaldts were at a loss as to how to help him. Then, while listening to the radio one night, they heard a program hosted by a UFO investigator. The investigator, W.K. (Bill) Allen, paid a visit to the Seewaldt home a few nights later. He spoke with Angela and interviewed David extensively, trying to note every detail the boy could remember. After he left, David felt calmer and the whole family believed that at least, they had done something. The family returned to a normal routine but it only lasted five months.

The quiet was shattered one night in April when David had a horrible dream. He struggled in his sleep, thrashing about and moaning loudly as if he was in pain. When a family member was finally able to wake him, he quickly stated he remembered what had happened to him. "Call Dad" he said. "There were monsters," he said, and they had taken him aboard the flying saucer.

Bill Allen was called back to the family's home. Allen began working with David and the family to help get to the root of what David had experienced that November night. He suggested a series of hypnotic regressions to help the young man recover his lost memories of the incident. Allen enlisted the help of a dentist named Dr. Kimball, who was well versed in hypnosis. Kimball used hypnosis frequently to help his patients and he had worked with Allen on other cases.

Kimball, with Allen present, began to take David through the standard relaxation stages to induce a hypnotic state. He guided the boy back to the night in question, November 17, 1967. Taking David through some of the memories of his time after school with his friend Matt, Kimball brought David to the moment in the field when he saw the saucer. Suddenly, the hypnotized boy could not answer any questions. His legs began to shake violently and fear racked his body. The doctor calmed the boy and brought him back out of the trance. Subsequent sessions only led to the same results. Once the young man recalled seeing the silver saucer in the sky, he became immobilized with fear and no further information could be obtained.

Allen was now even more convinced that David had experienced something traumatic on the evening in November. After several sessions, Dr. Kimball decided to alter his approach. A different technique, he reasoned, may be needed to get beyond David's terror. The doctor suggested that David view the entire incident as though he was watching it on television, reminding him that he had never been hurt watching television and that nothing could possibly harm him now. Allen and Kimball called in a psychologist from the University of Alberta, Dr. Masson, to assist with the sessions.

Under deep hypnosis, and now just watching the events that had happened, David was able to answer questions about what had occurred in the field. The boy reported seeing a large, silver saucer in the sky above him. The craft had colored lights all around it. He reported seeing blue, red, green, pink, yellow and orange lights all coming from the ship. When asked what happened, David said an orange beam shot out from the bottom of the craft and shone on him. Pressed for details of what happened when the light hit him, David said he felt like he was in a trance and couldn't move. Next, he felt the beam pulling him, causing him to rise up off the ground. The light pulled him all the way up and took him inside the flying saucer. Inside, he reported, were monsters. The doctor asked David to describe the beings that he was seeing.

"They're scary. They have eyes that go around the side of their heads, and they only have holes where their ears and nose should be. They're brown. They just keep staring at me, not saying anything."

"How many monsters are there?" the doctor asked. David replied that there were two. The doctor also asked the young man to describe what kind of clothing the creatures were wearing. The boy reported the creatures were not wearing any clothing at all and they had rough, brown skin like that of a crocodile. The hypnotists then asked David if the beings also had a back like a crocodile.

"I never saw their backs" the boy replied. Further questions revealed the creatures were about the size of David's father. They didn't seem to express any emotion. Not anger or happiness, just a cold stare. The aliens placed David on a low cot and undressed him. They then proceeded to take him down a hallway, into another room. Here, bright lights covered the ceiling. David then described what has become very typical in abduction scenarios; he was placed on an examination table while the crocodile beings worked around him. They made buzzing noises David believed to be the sound of them communicating with one another. The creatures only had a small slit where a mouth would normally be. In the brightly lit room, the aliens continued to examine the boy.

"He's lifting my head up. He's lifting it up! He looks at my hair and my eyes and my nose." Despite the deep hypnosis and the detached view, David was clearly having difficulty recounting this portion of his experience. At this point, David reported that he believed four of the creatures were present.

Further into the hypnosis session, David reported the creatures did something else:

"They put this other thing over me. It's a grayish color and they just throw it over me and then this great big, huge, orange-colored light comes down and is shown on me. Then one of them took sort of a needle. It's gray, it's small. He sticks it in my arm."

After the examination, the creatures dressed the boy and wheeled him to another part of the ship. They placed him in the orange beam of light, which transported him down to the field where he had been snatched. It was at this point David ran back to his home in a panic, all memories of the incident and the aliens lost until his dreams and sessions with the hypnotists revealed his experience with the crocodile aliens.

The Alligator Ship

"It was oblong, and the outer surface reminded me of alligator skin. It was rough looking. On top there was a dome and that's where the light was coming from." This was part of the description of a strange craft a man in Prince George, British Columbia, Canada, encountered in the summer of 1976.

The case was reported in the summer 1977 edition of *Canadian UFO Report*. Ottawa newspaper correspondent, reporter and UFO investigator, John Magor researched the case, dubbed "the highway incident." The case was originally discussed on Prince George radio station CJCI. Two men were present during the incident, and one of them appeared on the show. Initially the witness chose to be anonymous and simply went by "X." Magor later received permission to release the man's name. "X" turned out to be a gentleman named Kirk Alore, a supermarket employee who was driving a truck at the time of the encounter. Magor released the man's identity in a follow-up article in *Canadian UFO Report*, Winter-Summer 1978 edition. There had been quite a few sightings in the Prince George region of British Columbia in the summer of 1976, and this particular incident was especially interesting.

On July 5, Alore was driving his vehicle on highway 16 between Prince George and Vanderhoof. It was early morning and he was en route to Fort St. James. According to Alore, a mile before the incident, he looked at his watch and noted the time to be ten past four. He came to a straight stretch of road and noticed a red light in the sky. He then noticed a car coming towards him on the road ahead. The two vehicles were about three hundred yards apart when the red light dropped out of the sky and started moving towards Alore. Panicked, the driver swerved and suddenly found the interior of his truck illuminated with a red light. The radio died and the truck's engine shut off. Alore passed out.

At four-thirty, he was awakened by a man shaking him, asking if he was okay. It was the driver of the other vehicle. This man, too, had passed out but had regained consciousness on the road outside of his car. Alore himself was now sitting in the passenger side of his own vehicle, unsure how he had come to be there or exactly what had happened. Both men examined the road and searched for skid marks from their brakes, but none could be found. The two vehicles were no more than two feet apart. Alore said the other driver also reported that his engine had died, he had suddenly passed out and he could recall nothing until he awoke on the road.

Both men were thoroughly checked out at a hospital in

Vanderhoof. Reportedly, there were in a state of shock but nothing else was physically wrong with them. Alore failed to get the other man's name, likely due to the confused state that he was in. Further interviews with Alore did reveal some other, interesting details about the craft he spotted at the onset of the incident. In describing the object, he stated:

"To me it looked like a giant lizard with wings, and it was a little over one and a half times the size of the road width. I don't think it was like anything we could build. That's how strange it looked and that's what scared me. It didn't look like anything I had seen before, except maybe the lizard part. That's about the only thing I could relate it to." Alore further stated the craft had wings that looked like "frog legs spread out, with that gap in them." He was not able to see any engines on the craft. He reported the craft was oblong in shape and the outer shell or surface resembled alligator skin. It also had small, rounded, protruding wings. Between the wings was a circular shape that resembled an electric razor. On top of the ship was a dome from which the light emitted. Like the David Seewaldt case, the dome had multi-colored lights, red, yellow, blue and green. The red light formed a straight beam that shone directly on Alore's truck.

Alore reported that he had never experienced blackouts before in his life and had no history of passing out. When the beam hit him however, it caused him to lose consciousness:

"It felt as if there were a bunch of pins in me, and then I sort of went into nothing. The last thing I remember was my motor dying, my radio going funny and seeing this guy not more than a hundred yards away and heading straight for me. I was doing at least seventy miles an hour. I remember putting my foot on the brake, but there were no skid marks."

Alore also asserted he had not been drinking and was not tired. He had, in fact, pulled over on the side of the road farther south that night and slept for somewhere between two and three hours. When he continued his drive, he was rested, wide-awake, and had his radio playing at full blast. Still, Alore could not explain the incident or what he saw and experienced. He has no idea how he lost time or how he ended up in the passenger seat of his own vehicle. When asked if he believed in UFOs, Alore responded:

"I do now. I didn't before, but I do now."

Chapter Five Grinning Men, Reptoids and Cold Characters

Chapter Six
Hiding in Human Form

Not Quite Human

People have long been fascinated with legends of shapeshifters and otherworldly beings that are seemingly *almost* human. Diverse cultures from around the world have such beings in their traditional lore. Sometimes they are good, often they are evil, hiding among 'normal' humans until they decide to change, or are forced to. Such stories are in part the inspiration for werewolves and other classic horror tales. It's really something to be confronted with a fear that 'has teeth' so to speak. You know what I mean, the creatures that haunt classic horror movies; fur covered, deathly pale with claws, giant teeth or tentacles. These are the obvious monsters that mean harm and have no qualms about showing their intent and their true nature. But there are other things out there that are more subtle. Are there monsters among us? Are there beings that are simply hiding in human form, waiting for the proper moment to show their true colors? The accounts in this chapter will leave many shaking their heads, believing it's all nonsense; others will approach the accounts with a more open mind and wonder if such things are truly out there. Still others may perhaps feel a chill as they recall similar incidents in their own lives and question whether or not if what they thought was a person —was really a human being at all.

The Presence of Evil

Robert told me about a strange experience he had while living in the Hawaiian Islands:

"I have to tell somebody about this; I've held it in for far too long. What I'm about to tell you is the absolute truth. God knows. Today I live on the west coast, but in the 1980s I was living in Hawaii, trying to take it easy after some intense years and a lot of travel. The Hawaiian Islands are beautiful and I was living in a sparsely populated valley. Not long after moving there, I met a couple named Tom and Ann. They lived on the other side of the river from me so either I would have to walk down to the bridge and walk up the road to their property or I had to go across the river. Nevertheless, it was in the jungle and there were no streetlights. We used flashlights or lighters to walk through it at night.

Tom and Ann seemed to be nice people, very hospitable and Tom was a musician who played guitar and wrote songs, so we got along well. He also had a vast knowledge of plants and had the most beautiful garden I had ever seen. Ann was a wonderful cook. I went over there daily and we became good friends. I did find it weird that they hardly had any other friends or visitors, and Tom always acted like they were hiding from someone or something. They definitely had a strange side to them but I didn't pry.

One night after I'd already lived there for several months, I was over at their house as usual, sitting at the table enjoying food and conversation. I was eating, looking down at my plate, Tom and Ann were saying something, when all of a sudden, like a switch went off, they stopped talking in mid-sentence. I looked up from my plate across the table at Tom sitting, and Ann standing next to him, and I saw them there, as if frozen in time. Their mouths were wide open with their eyes and their mouths completely black. And I don't mean normal black. I mean a deep, empty black. Blacker than a black you've ever seen in your life. Almost like another dimensional black. Their mouths as black as their eyes. You could feel the black (if that makes any sense).

I was immediately struck with a sense of fear. As I stood up and looked at them, I couldn't believe what I was seeing. I wasn't high, I wasn't drinking, I was just seeing something that I couldn't understand. I sat back down, contemplating running through that dark jungle full of fear to get home, when everything returned to normal, like a light switch turned back on. It was as if nothing had happened at all. The whole episode lasted about fifteen seconds, maybe longer; I was in shock. So I got a good chance to make sure what I was seeing was really what I was seeing.

After everything returned to normal, I was left with extreme fear and that overwhelming sense that I needed to get out of there. Tom and Ann asked what was wrong and I said, "I'm sorry, I just have to go, I-I have to leave. I have to go." It would prove to be a long, scary walk back home through the jungle. I did not go over there for weeks after that and only saw them occasionally. I never told them what I saw, how could I? Even until this day, I've hardly told anyone. The overwhelming sense I had during this episode was extreme fear and of being in the presence of evil."

Recently Robert has been trying to put the pieces together and understand, or at least come to terms with what he witnessed. Since his encounter in the 1980s, Robert has been haunted by the experience. "It still scares the hell out of me when I think about it" he reports. "Something is going on...this is real!"

Not long after his weird experience, Robert left Hawaii. Strangely enough, he found he suddenly developed an extreme fear of heights. He also began to experience panic attacks while driving. Is this connected to his encounter with the two strange people? Did the extreme fear Robert felt when peering into the black voids somehow stay with him?

Fear in the Aftermath

As it turns out, Robert is not the only one to experience strange side effects or changes in his nature after having this type of experience. Take the case of Marcel. I met Marcel when I was speaking at the Sacramento UFO/Paranormal Summit. He told me his story about a bizarre couple that lived in his apartment building in New York City. "I don't believe they were human, but they were hiding in human form," Marcel told me.

In 2010, Marcel was living in an apartment building in New York City. During the fall of that year, he had an encounter with a strange couple whose eyes turned solid black.

"I was living in a downtown apartment, my place was on the third floor. I moved in at the beginning of the year and it wasn't long before I noticed that there was a fairly high turnover at the place. I'll be honest, it wasn't a great place. It was old and run-down but it was what I could afford at the time and even then, I had to have a roommate. My roommate traveled a lot though, so more often than not, I had the whole place to myself.

It was in the fall when this guy moved in across the hall from

101

me. His name was Jeff; I never knew his last name. He seemed a bit reclusive, a loner type and he never wanted to talk when I saw him in the hallway. He would just mumble hi and go into his apartment. I figured that he worked from home or something because he was just always there. He kept his television on day and night; I don't think it was ever turned off. Suddenly, one day, there was a young woman who came out of his apartment. She was Asian and I guessed that she was in her twenties just like Jeff appeared to be. I said hello to her and she looked at me kind of strange. She replied, "I stay here," pointing at the apartment door. I found this odd too, but thought maybe she just didn't speak much English. The other odd thing was that instead of leaving, she watched me walk down the hallway. When I reached the steps, I turned and looked back to see if she was coming. She was staring at me; then she suddenly went back into the apartment and slammed the door. I thought maybe I had scared her or something by trying to talk to her.

I didn't see either one of them for the next couple of weeks, but they were constantly having takeout delivered. Pizza, Chinese, you name it. I figured they didn't cook at all, just ate out all the time. Honestly, I sort of wondered where they got the money for it because eating that way all the time is pretty expensive.

A little more time went by and it was getting close to the holidays. I lost my job at the beginning of November because the company I worked for closed. I knew it was coming ahead of time so I had saved enough money to pay the next couple of months' rent. By then my lease would be up and I was moving to Boston for another job. My roommate came back for a couple of weeks and one night we were sitting around having some drinks. He asked me, "What's up with the weird couple across the hall?" I wanted to hear his opinion on them so I asked what he meant.

"Well, I ran into the two of them a few nights ago and said hello, they practically ran away from me and they seem really weird about anyone seeing into their apartment. A college friend of mine delivered a pizza there yesterday. He said they went out of their way to make sure he couldn't see into the apartment."

We talked about all the different possibilities. They acted paranoid, but it didn't seem like they were drug dealers because they rarely went out and the only people who ever came by were food delivery guys, many of whom we knew personally.

My roommate left again to visit family for the Thanksgiving

holiday so I was alone at the apartment again. It was two days before Thanksgiving. I had come home after having coffee with a couple of friends at a nearby coffee shop. It was fairly cold and I was walking quick, getting up the stairs so I could get inside and warm up. I reached my floor and turned the corner quickly into the hallway. There was Jeff and his girlfriend right by their door. It seemed like I really shocked them when I came around the corner. She was carrying a couple of grocery bags and dropped one of them when she saw me, some of the contents fell out into the hallway. She gave me a really dirty look as if I had caused it. Jeff was fumbling with the keys getting their door unlocked. I tried to smile and apologized, bending down to pick up some of the contents to help her. It was all different kinds of canned meat. I mean, there was nothing else, no bread, no household items, just a bunch of cans of meat- Spam, potted meat, deviled ham, canned fish, you name it.

Just as I was trying to help pick the stuff up, Jeff turned, looked down at me and said in an angry tone, "Just leave it! She'll get it." I looked up at him and I swear, in that moment, his eyes were solid black, no whites in his eyes at all. I realized that the girl was staring at me too and when I looked over at her, her eyes were solid black just like his. I was pretty close to her because we were both bending down picking stuff up. There's no way it was a trick of the light or anything. I just stared at her and looked at those solid, black eyes; it was the most disturbing thing. While I was looking at her, I saw her eyes turn back to regular, brown eyes with whites around them. It all must have happened within a few seconds. Suddenly, Jeff had the door open and they both rushed inside, leaving some of the canned meat on the floor in the hallway. I got into my apartment as quick as I could, I was really shaken up. I called some friends who I was going to be seeing for Thanksgiving; they had offered to let me come over and stay a couple of days and now I decided to take them up on it. I quickly packed a bag and left. When I left the apartment, I noticed that all the canned meat was gone; perhaps they had slipped out and picked it all up.

I stayed with my friends longer than I intended, I was still too disturbed to go home. Finally, on the Monday after Thanksgiving, I went back to my apartment. The first thing I noticed was that the television wasn't on in Jeff's apartment. The thing had run 24/7 and now it was off so it was quite a change. A couple of days passed and I realized that no delivery people had been around to drop off food. When I went to drop off my rent check, I asked the landlord if he knew anything about Jeff and his girlfriend. He was rather irritated at the mention and simply told me that they had ditched out on the lease and moved out in the middle of the night one night. He had no idea where they had gone."

After the run-in with Jeff and his girlfriend, Marcel started experiencing some changes. First he developed claustrophobia. Marcel had never been afraid of small spaces, and in fact remembers often hiding in a closet under the stairs growing up. He would pretend it was a secret cave and spend hours there. Now he found himself not only afraid of small spaces, but feeling panic set in after just a moment in tight quarters.

The other effect was even stranger; he became an unwilling vegetarian. Growing up and throughout his life, Marcel had a diet heavy in meat, yet soon after his encounter, he found he couldn't stomach it.

"The first thing was that right after seeing the weird-eyed couple, I got sick after eating some fried chicken. I was sick all through the holidays; it was tough. I thought it was a case of food poisoning and it took me several days to recover. I was hardly eating during that time because I just couldn't keep anything down. After I was feeling normal and felt like I could eat regular meals, I had eggs and sausage for breakfast one morning. I got sick right after. It lasted the whole day. I got checked out by the doctor, but they couldn't find anything wrong with me. So I tried to just continue on like things were normal but I kept getting sick. A friend of mine suggested that I start adding one item a day to my food until I hit the thing that made me sick. I ate toast one day, then added bananas, then something else. I was fine until I added chicken and got really sick. This process went on for some time, every time I added some kind of meat, I was very sick. Beef, pork, fish, it all makes me sick now so I've become a vegetarian even though I didn't want to."

Did Marcel have some kind of psychological reaction after witnessing the strange couple and all their canned meat products? It is possible since he was so disturbed by the incident but it is an extreme reaction, and why did their eyes shift in such a manner?

"I think their anger made them drop their guard. I don't think they were human, but they were hiding in human form. I hope I never experience something like that again."

Behind the Blinds in Suburbia

The account below is from Charlene in Florida. Charlene's story is similar to other accounts I've been receiving of seemingly normal people whose eyes suddenly turn solid black. Often the witness has known the person for some time and may have noticed unusual behavior. Charlene relates her account:

"We live in an area where a lot of the houses are rentals. The house next door to ours sat empty for quite some time until a couple finally rented it. Their names were Chad and Beth. They didn't have any kids, which put them in the minority for our neighborhood. Since they were right next door, my husband and I ended up talking to them often. They would never really talk about what they did for a living, just that they worked from home on the computer. They certainly seemed nice and normal at first. About six months after knowing them, we began to notice some strange things, here are a couple of them: First of all, one day we were grilling out. We invited several people over and included Chad and Beth. They came to the cookout but my husband and I both noticed that they stayed far away from the grill. We assumed they both must have been afraid of fire but they wouldn't even go near it after it was closed. Right after that cookout, Beth started coming over to visit during the day when my husband was at work. She would look around the house constantly, like she was examining everything. It started to make me very uncomfortable. She wasn't much for conversation and there never really seemed to be a point to her visits. I mentioned it to my husband but he assumed she was just bored and wanted company. After a week of these visits, I didn't see her for a few days. That weekend, I brought my mother's cat to our house. My mother was going on vacation and wanted us to watch her cat for her. The next day, Beth came for one of her visits. She sat in the same kitchen chair, the only place she would seem to sit. Ten minutes after she had been there the cat came out of the bedroom. The cat went crazy when she saw Beth. The cat's hair stood up and she let out a loud hiss. Beth leaned forward and looked at the cat with a really nasty look. The cat ran back to the bedroom and Beth just stood up and left without saying a word. The whole thing was so strange to me. When my husband got home, I told him the story. He decided that we should go over and visit Chad and Beth. We walked over to their house and knocked on the door. As we stood on the steps, there were such strange noises coming from inside. There was a loud crash like something had been thrown against the wall and then all of a sudden the door opened and they were both standing there like everything was normal. We started to talk to them, expecting to be invited inside but they just stood there side by side. I asked Beth if she was okay and said, "I didn't realize you were afraid of cats." Chad shot her a look very suddenly and he looked angry. It was clear that Beth was very nervous and she wouldn't say anything. It was a very awkward moment. Chad looked like he was getting more and more angry. Beth wouldn't look at him and my husband and I didn't know what to say. I was looking at Beth and she glanced at me. When she did, her eyes suddenly went from normal blue eyes to solid black. I felt my jaw drop, then I felt my husband pulling on my arm and we were rushing across the lawn back to our house. When we got inside, I asked my husband if he saw Beth's eyes change. He answered, "Yes, and so did Chad's!" Both their eyes went solid black and in that moment, we both felt the need to run away from them. The next day, whenever we were outside, we would notice that Chad or Beth were looking out at us from behind their blinds. A week later, we realized that they had moved away but it must have been late at night since no one saw them move out."

Following up on this strange account, I discovered that in fact, no one in the neighborhood had seen the couple move out of the house. Furthermore, no one could recall seeing them move in either. They were just there — acting as if they had lived in the house all along. In a normal suburban community this doesn't make any sense. While people move in and out of houses on a regular basis, the process usually involves packing and moving trucks. Vanishing in the middle of the night implies criminal activity, but there was never any evidence of illegal actions. While other people living in the area had noticed strange behavior from Chad and Beth, there were no other witnesses who saw the couple's eyes shift to a different color.

What we are left with is an odd puzzle, seemingly without all the pieces. The feeling that Charlene and her husband experienced when confronting the weird couple has haunted them for some time.

"The cat incident, the weird things they would say and those eyes changing into solid black, I don't know what they were, but I just don't think they were really human" Charlene says.

In recent years there's been much talk about the so-called 'Reptilians'. These creatures are reputed to be bipedal humanoid creatures with reptilian features. Varying descriptions of these beings show them as having lizard-like skin, large, bulging eyes and large lizard-shaped heads. Those who report encounters with these creatures claim the reptilians have arms and legs like a human but with reptile-like hands and feet.

Perhaps even more disturbing, many people believe these reptilians are able to hide among us in human form. It seems there are constant tales of reptilians lurking around us. Even popular media has tapped into the idea with movie and television versions of reptilians bent on conquering, and possibly even eating humans. It certainly sounds like the stuff of pure science fiction. Why then, do so many people believe the reptilians actually exist? Does it tap into some ancient, primal fear of reptiles? Let's face it, for those afraid of snakes, could there be anything worse than one in human form hiding out as a typical man on the street?

Some people find the whole thing laughable, but there are a couple of factors to consider. First, tales of bipedal reptoids have been around for a long, long time, and second, the stories are still turning up continually. Not all of the people who report such things are crackpots or delusional. Some are simply trying to understand what they saw and why it was not quite...human.

Take the account from John, a logical guy, retired computer expert, with a fairly normal life. That is, until a very odd family moved to his neighborhood.

The Snakeheads Move In

"For several years in the early 2000s, I lived in a house just outside of Dayton, Ohio. It was a quiet area, mostly working class people and the houses were pretty reasonable, cost-wise. I was living on a street where most of the homes had a good-sized yard. The people mostly kept to themselves, but would speak to you if you were outside in the yard or walking around. I had a huge front yard and it seemed like I had to mow it constantly. I would often speak to my next-door neighbor on a casual basis. He had a small plumbing company and honestly, we didn't really have anything in common. My background was computers and he wasn't interested in that at all. Still, he seemed to know everything about the neighborhood. I think because his wife was so nosy and kept up with all the local news.

About five houses down from mine, there was an empty ranch house. When I was looking for a house myself, the realtor mentioned it to me. She said that it had sat empty for a good while and that I could probably get it pretty easy and cheap. When I asked why, she told me that the people who used to live there had been foreclosed on and had torn the inside of the house up. They busted all the fixtures and ripped holes in the walls. I wasn't interested in having to deal with that kind of repair so I didn't even look at the place. It was almost a year after I moved into my house before someone moved into the ranch home. The weird thing was I saw these people moved in very suddenly. I didn't see any workers at the house making repairs. I thought, well, the guy must plan to do it all himself.

Of course, my next-door neighbor and his wife had a lot to say about it. My neighbor had stopped by and offered his card, along with a discount on some of the plumbing work that needed done in the house. He said that the man stood blocking his view inside the house but he could see a little. "There were just some mattresses on the floor of the living room, no furniture," he told me. The man took the business card and just looked at it for a moment, then handed it back saying there was nothing that needed done in the home. With that, he closed the door.

I started seeing the new people on a regular basis when I was out walking my dog. It was my habit to take the dog around on a course of several blocks, down to a park and then back to my house. It would be about five-thirty when I was walking down our street and I would see this guy pull up in his old car. It was a beater and sounded like it was barely running. The guy usually wore some pretty worn out clothing so I figured they didn't have a whole lot of money. The car was always full of trash. I mean, really full, overflowing in the back seats, you couldn't have sat back there for all of the trash. I would always say hello but this guy never responded to me. Finally, I got to where I just wouldn't say anything because I knew he wouldn't respond.

I ran into him one night at the nearby Meijer's grocery store. He was in the meat department and he had a cart that was slam full of meats; from what I could see, it was all beef, lots of hamburger, steaks, and so forth. He looked up and saw me looking into his shopping cart and gave me a nasty look. I said hello to him and commented, "You must be having a barbecue." He looked like I had slapped him; I've never seen such a look. He opened his mouth and made sort of a hissing sound, just weird, like the air being forced out of his teeth. He turned around and stormed away and I saw him head to the checkout. I just didn't know what to make of the incident. It had me curious though and the next day when I saw my next-door neighbor, I had to bring up the strange people. "Don't get me started on them," he said. When I asked what he meant, he told me that his wife would not stop talking about them. He told me that his wife claimed to see the woman outside in the back yard, chasing a cat. The cat got away and this lady was really angry about it. "Here's the kicker though," he said. "My wife says that lady was wearing a wig and that it fell off. When it did, she said the woman's head is bald and scaled like a snake's." He went on to tell me that his wife had become obsessed with the idea that they were reptiles and that she was constantly reading about such things on the Internet. He was worried that his wife was really losing it.

I'm just a curious guy by nature, probably to my detriment sometimes, but now I was really curious about these people. I decided to try a little experiment the next night. I started walking my dog and took my time until I saw the old car pulling up. I got to the guy just as he was crossing the sidewalk to go into his house and let my dog's lead out some. My dog ran forward, but when he got close to this guy, he turned and ran back to me. I stepped up right beside the man. He wouldn't say anything to me even when I pressed at him and he averted his eyes away from me. When he turned, I noticed that he was wearing a toupee. I was flabbergasted. Not only was he wearing a headpiece, but coming from underneath it, on his neck, there was what looked like very dried skin, it almost looked like scales. 'My God,' I thought, Could my neighbor's wife be right? Were these people not people at all?"

John threw himself into research, and like most people these days turned to the Internet. What he found was a massive amount of information, speculation and dialogue about the so-called reptilians. He spent time talking to his neighbor's wife to get the details about her account directly from her. She had convinced herself that reptilians were in their midst and that they were working to take over the country.

"She spent all her time watching videos on the Internet and reading material from authors who are convinced there's some grand reptilian conspiracy to take over the planet. She even took to calling the weird neighbors the snakeheads."

John had a number of other experiences related to the weird family. Besides the husband and wife, there were two other older boys that lived in the house. John and others assumed they were 'children' of the couple. They rarely went outside the house, and like their father never spoke to anyone.

"There was a teenage boy from the neighborhood that I started paying to cut my grass. He'd been doing it for awhile and we would often chat about football since we were both big fans. One day he looked at me very serious and asked if I knew anything about the people down the street. When I asked him why, he told me that he had stopped by their house and offered to cut their grass. One of the boys had opened the door and just shook his head no. "I could see their kitchen table," he told me. "They were all sitting there and I swear they were eating raw meat."

The odd family lived in the neighborhood for a year and a half. One day, they all piled into the old car and left, never to be seen again. John happened to catch a work truck in front of the house one day and stopped to see what was going on. It was a cleanup crew sent by the realty company.

"I went in and just started talking to the workers. The place was a total wreck. There were old mattresses on the floor with just a dirty sheet on them. There was a dining room table that was roughly nailed together; it looked like it came from a dump. All the holes were still in the walls. There weren't even any toilets, just the holes in the floors where they had been. There was fecal matter on the floors of the bathroom. In the kitchen there was trash everywhere; most of it was from meat packages. The stench was overwhelming."

Being a self-proclaimed 'rational thinker' John spent time trying to find logical reasons to explain away the incidents he and others had noted around the family. He found the reptilian theories on the Internet too extreme and too far outside of his traditional belief systems. Still, he is left with many unanswered questions.

"Honestly, I just didn't know what to think. The neighborhood was not the same while those people lived there. Everyone just seemed uneasy. A lot of people had seen strange things but I don't know if it was all coincidental or if something else was going on. I still have a hard time bringing myself to accept that they were some kind of reptiles but I can't deny how weird it all was."

The jury is out on what John was dealing with. While he hasn't accepted the people were aliens or reptoids, he is open to all possibilities. As he stated, "If they were human, they certainly weren't normal people. If they were something else, well, I'm just glad they went away."

In her book, *The Djinn Connection*, author Rosemary Ellen Guiley draws many comparisons between the djinn and the reptilians noting:

"Ancient drawings of the Djinn depict them as half-human, half-reptilian in form with clawed hands, horns and reptilian eyes."

The djinn of course are able to shapeshift into different forms and they could, in theory, take on the form of a normal human, or a bipedal, human-reptilian creature. Whether the reptilians are indeed djinn or something else remains to be seen but there is no doubt that people have spoken of their existence through the ages. In discussing the reptilians, Guiley points out:

"Whatever they are, intelligent reptilians, especially in humanoid form, have a long presence on the planet, and people have encountered them. Two main types have emerged in the literature: the reptoids, a subterranean hybrid of reptilian in humanoid form, and the extraterrestrial Dracos, who also are a combination of reptile and human forms. The reptoids may be an ancient race that has lived below the surface of the earth, sharing the planet with humans for millennia. Both types are associated with ET and UFO activity, and play a role in ET abductions, usually along with grays, and also gray-reptilian hybrids."

The connection between the reptilians and the alien grays has long been discussed. While the reptilians are almost universally seen as a sinister presence, opinions on the grays is a bit divided. The reptilian connection is a difficult thing to reconcile for those who believe the grays are a benevolent race here to help our planet. And what about the so-called alien hybrid breeding program? Countless abductees report they have been subjected to an extraterrestrial breeding process. But why would another race want or need to breed with humans? Often, abductees report seeing the offspring that result from this program, usually during a later abduction experience aboard a spacecraft. Some reports have emerged though, that indicate the presence of alien hybrids here on the planet with us. Was this the plan all along? Has the program taken a turn and are aliens now sending hybrids to live among us? Our next account may indicate this possibility.

"We're Half Way There"

The following is an account I received from a woman new to the UFO phenomenon. She had a strange experience while traveling in Colorado, and believes she encountered an alien-human hybrid.

Being a newcomer to the study of UFOs, she is still having difficulty coming to terms with many of the concepts and ideas she is now exploring. She finds herself overwhelmed with the scope of the field and its diverse personalities and theories. The field of ufology is, after all, a bit of a subculture, and she's still learning how to navigate it. She was thrown into the subject very suddenly when she learned her sister was an abductee.

Justine had not seen her older sister for over three years. When they finally reconnected in the spring of 2012, Justine received the surprise of her life. Her sister Catherine introduced her to the world of UFOs, aliens and abductees.

"Our parents separated when my sister and I were teenagers. As a result, we never felt that close to our parents because we just held a lot of anger towards them," recounts Justine. "I think it made my sister and I closer though. That's why it was hard when she just sort of disappeared on me. When she told me I wouldn't hear from her for awhile, I though she meant a few weeks, not several years. At first, I was irritated by it, then I was upset, which turned into me feeling really, really hurt. All kinds of things would go through my head, wondering if she was even still alive. Finally, I started getting so focused on my life, it sort of went to the back of my head and I didn't think about it as often."

Justine's sister finally got in touch with her in early 2012. She reported that she was living in Colorado and she wanted Justine to come visit her as soon as she could. It took a couple of months to arrange time off, but by the spring Justine was on the road to Colorado.

"Seeing Catherine was comfortable and tense at the same time. All the anger and worry that had built up over the time we had been out of contact came back to me. I arrived late on Thursday night and we talked well into the night. Mostly about old memories and then a lot about what I had done the past few years. I did start to relax and I just couldn't bring myself to stay angry once we were together again. When I started pressing her about what she had been doing all that time, she pushed me off to bed and said we'd talk tomorrow."

It wasn't until Friday night that Catherine dropped the bombshell on her sister.

"Justine. I'm an abductee."

Justine wasn't interested in UFOs and she didn't know what her sister was talking about when she made the statement. At first, she thought that her sister meant that she had been abducted by a person or group, perhaps a cult of some kind. It was a long conversation before she understood that Catherine was claiming to have been abducted, multiple times, by aliens.

"Outside of seeing a few movies, I've never paid any attention to all of the alien stuff. It took quite a while before I got that my sister was serious and that she really believed that she had been abducted by creatures in UFOs. Catherine had moved to Colorado to get away and focus on herself and her experiences. She told me that the abductions had been going on for many years and that when memories started coming back, she felt a need to withdraw and try to understand it all. We talked about her experiences for most of the rest of the weekend and I asked a lot of questions. Before I left, she gave me a few books to read, two books by Stan Romanek, *Messages* and *Answers*, and a couple by Whitley Strieber, apparently, the most famous abductee.

Honestly, I still wasn't sure what to make of the whole thing. I mean, we were suddenly talking about beings from outer space and all I could think about were cartoons of little green men from Mars. I wondered if this was all real somehow or if my sister had gone off some deep end. If she had cracked, she could believe all of the crazy alien stuff. But when I left I promised her that I would read through the books and that I would visit again in the summer. She was hoping that I would accept what had happened to her and that we could be close again. I just wasn't sure where it was all going."

Justine headed home, driving south through Colorado. It was a long trip, but she was making good time. She had called her work and asked for some extra time off so she didn't have to be back at work for two days. She reasoned the extra time would allow her an opportunity to take her time driving and try to come to grips with her sister's revelations. It was mid-afternoon when she pulled into a gas station just off the interstate to refuel and grab something to drink.

"I stopped at a gas station to fill up the tank. I'll admit, my mind was a million miles away at the time. With everything that my sister had dropped on me my thoughts were just racing. I was sort of on autopilot when I pulled up to the pump and got out of the car. I ran my credit card, put the nozzle in and started pumping gas. All of a sudden, I realized there was a young girl standing there. She was near the front of my car on the little island where the pumps sit. Even though I was distracted, I don't know how I missed seeing her when I pulled up. She was wearing a cream-colored dress that looked rather old to me. I thought, well, it's Sunday, maybe she's been to church. I don't even know why I was thinking about it. She was standing there staring at me and I looked right at her. She had the most startling blue eyes that I have ever seen. I think her pupils must have been really large and it made her eyes look oversized. I couldn't even see any whites in her eyes from where I was, just that bright blue. She looked fairly normal otherwise. Her hair was very pale blonde and her skin was extremely white as if she never got any sun. I said hello to her but instead of saying hi back, she said:

"We're halfway there."

I wondered what in the world she meant by that. I said to her, "I don't understand." I looked around, expecting to see a car on the other side of the island because her parents had to be around. There was no one there. The little girl was still looking at me and she said, "Your sister Catherine will understand; it's for all of us." It gave me a chill.

I let go of the gas nozzle and started to walk towards her. She didn't move, but I only took a couple of steps before I felt like I shouldn't go any closer. All of a sudden, I was kind of afraid. I stepped back, put the nozzle back in the pump and opened my car door. The little girl, still watching me, said again, "We're halfway there." Just at that moment, a pickup truck pulled up at the pumps to my right. I looked over and saw an older man get out of his truck. I called out, "Excuse me" and he turned towards me saying "Yeah?" and I glanced towards the little girl. I just wanted this man to see her and see if she would say something to him. She was gone. I looked around and she was nowhere in sight. I turned back towards the man with my mouth hanging open. He was just looking at me. I knew he hadn't seen the girl. I muttered that I was sorry, jumped in my car and drove away."

Justine was very shaken by her encounter at the gas station. Once she calmed down some, she called her sister and told her about the little girl who had mentioned her by name.

"You've seen a hybrid," Catherine told her. Justine had been introduced to the concept of alien-human hybrids during the weekend with her sister. It wasn't something they had discussed in depth, because Justine was trying to accept the simple idea her sister had been abducted. The possibility of alien children was a far stretch for someone new to the concepts she had been confronted with, especially the idea that aliens were somehow using humans to breed. Catherine had said a lot of abductees were being taken because of their use in a hybrid breeding program of some kind. Although her sister had hinted at something like this having happened to her, she couldn't bring herself to ask questions about it.

"Maybe it was a hybrid, I don't know. I don't think that girl could have vanished like that but I don't think I was imagining things either. I do believe she was real and what she said has stuck in my mind. What did she mean when she said half-way there? Half-way to what? From the way the girl stated it, it wasn't just about Catherine and I, but about people in general. My sister and I have discussed it many times but we don't have an answer yet."

The child's statement remains a mystery at this time. Neither of the sisters could think of anything on a personal level to help them understand the phrase. Justine is certainly not the first person to encounter what they believe to be an alien hybrid. It's interesting to hear accounts from those new to the world of UFOs. There's no preconceived idea or agenda to promote, just a strange encounter to relate, and attempt to understand. Of course Justine was thrown fully into the world of aliens and abductions. In the months following her sister's revelations, the two women started to spend more time together. Justine began to open up about a series of strange memories that had haunted her for a long time. The memories involved bright lights, large, oversized jackrabbits and missing time.

Catherine always believed her sister was also an abductee and she believes their experiences go back to childhood:

"One of the reasons that I had to disappear and not have contact with Justine for a time was that I wanted to understand my abduction experience without dragging her into it. But the more memories that came forth, the more I realized that we had both been taken since we were young girls. It took me a long while to finally contact her because I knew that once I opened up, it might cause some of her own memories to start to come back. That's exactly what has happened and it hasn't been easy for her. Together though, I think we'll be able to work through this and start to understand what it is all about."

Throughout history, we can find tales such as these — accounts of beings from other worlds, slipping into our reality and assuming human form in order to blend in. Ancient Celtic lore is rich with stories of changelings, fay children that are put in place of a stolen human child. Often, a long period would pass before anyone realized something was not quite right, not quite human.

During the middle ages, there was a terrible period of witch-hunts. Driven by the fear that people were in league with the devil, inquisitors devised elaborate, often torturous methods to 'detect' those practicing the black arts. Again, it was the primal fear that someone was not quite who or what they seemed to be.

In modern times, the accounts have evolved to stories of extraterrestrials who have come from a distant planet to interfere with the Earth. While some of them lurk just beyond the shadows, threatening the night with dreadful probes, others may have already become a force walking among us, normal in form and almost every detail, but yet, not quite human.

Is it all fanciful imagination or is there something more to these age-old tales and modern accounts? It may be a long time before we learn the answer, but in the meantime, it might be a good idea to pay attention to the little details. You never know when someone or something might slip up and reveal itself.

Chapter Seven
Black Eyed Beings

Those Terrible, Black Eyes

The black eyed kids, or BEKs, have become a hot topic in the field of paranormal studies. An encounter posted on the Internet in 1998 by journalist Brian Bethel instigated a modern wave of BEK accounts. Bethel's account rates as the most-recounted story of black eyed kids having been told and re-told on hundreds of Websites. The topic remains controversial with many people convinced the tales are merely a modern urban legend, mistaken identities or outright hoaxes. What can't be denied however, is the growing number of BEK accounts from every corner of the globe. People from all ages, races and geographical regions are reporting encounters with these weird kids. Numerous paranormal researchers have been collecting the accounts, and yet there are still few answers to the question of what exactly these children are.

When I did my own research on the BEKs I was intrigued to find older accounts that predated both the internet and television. These accounts fit the definite pattern of black eyed children encounters. Solid black eyes with no whites, pale skin and a monotone manner of speaking are all hallmarks of typical BEK accounts. In a 'standard' encounter, a person will arrive home from work and busy themselves about their home. A knock comes at the door. It's always a knock, the BEKs it seems, have not mastered the use of the doorbell. When the 'victim' answers the door, they find one or two children standing on their steps. The children will begin asking for an invitation inside. Using cryptic phrases such as "Just let us in; this won't take long," and other equally disturbing statements, the children will become insistent. At some point during the encounter, the children will look up and make eye contact, at which point the victim will realize the kids have solid black eyes. Once eye contact has been made, the victim finds their nervous, uneasy feeling has escalated to outright fear; flight response eventually kicks in and the victim gets away from the BEK

119

as quickly as possible. Those who have encountered the black eyed children experience a wide range of aftereffects including disturbed sleep patterns, nightmares, nervousness and even paranoia. It should also be noted the children are not limited to showing up at homes. People have been approached while sitting in their cars in parking lots, confronted at their place of work and even while out walking around their neighborhood. BEKs have shown up at hotel rooms, boats and countless other places.

The jury is still way out on what these beings actually are. The most popular theory by far is they are alien-human hybrids. The shiny, black eyes are of course most noted as evidence to support this contention. "It's like those alien grays," many witnesses have stated. Indeed, there is a stunning commonality between the classical depiction of the gray aliens and the black eyed children. Additionally, many people who claim to have experienced abduction by aliens believe the BEKs are the result of a long-running, alien hybrid breeding program. Many of these 'abductees' claim to have seen hybrid children during their periods of abduction on alien craft.

The second most popular theory to explain the children comes from a more religious perspective, that the BEKs are likely demons or of a demonic origin. The evidence to support this belief lies in part, once again, in the eyes. Demonologists contend a demonic entity cannot take on human form without something being distorted or malformed. In this case it would appear the beings appear like human children in every respect, save for the eyes. Religious believers profess the children are a demonic force, and this is why they create such a high level of fear in their victims. The other piece of evidence often cited to support the demon theory is the children always insist on an invitation inside. Again, demonologists have a reason for this. A demonic entity is unable to 'enter' —whether a home or a physical body— without an invitation. So far no accounts of a black eyed child forcing their way into a home have surfaced. This 'need' for an invitation inside is a component found in folklore around the world. Vampires, demons and other evil entities are said to be unable to cross a threshold without a proper invite. It seems a far stretch, but many aspects of classic folklore have been shown to have a basis in reality.

After my book on the BEKs was published, (*The Black Eyed Children*), I began to receive even more accounts from people around the world. Most were seeking answers to help them understand what they had encountered. While many of the cases were 'standard' accounts of BEKs showing up and attempting to gain entrance, some have stood out as different or unusual. I present a handful of these in this chapter.

BEK on the Balcony

Sandra encountered a black eyed kid while working in Florida. This particular child didn't show up at the front door however, rather 'he' took a more unconventional approach to try to gain entry into her apartment. Sandra recounts her experience:

"I was living in an apartment in the Miami, Florida area. I was doing a short-term project for a company in the city and they had rented me an executive apartment close to their corporate offices. It was a nice place, on the third floor as I had requested. The complex was secured and gated and they had their own security. The apartment was one bedroom, fully furnished and had a nice balcony off the living room. After several months, I had settled in and felt very secure.

I was working long hours, trying to wrap up the project I had been hired for. As a result, I would often come home in the late afternoon, grab a bite to eat and a couple of hours of sleep. After resting, I would put in a few hours doing computer work at my apartment.

I'll never forget what happened to me one Thursday afternoon. I had gone back to my apartment and was too tired to even make something to eat. I laid down on the couch and after a few minutes, I was out to the world. I believe I slept for about two hours when something woke me up. I had a strange feeling when I woke, and I thought that I'd heard a noise in my apartment. I just laid there on the couch, trying to wake up the rest of the way. I had my eyes open and I was looking around. I could see the clock on the wall and it was just after five. It was summer and there was still plenty of light outside and coming through the windows. After a moment, I realized what had caused me to wake up. Someone was knocking on the door. I kept laying there though, because the knock didn't sound quite right. I sat up on the couch, fully awake and listened to the knocking. I suddenly realized that the knocking was coming from behind me. My front door was across the room in front of me. The only thing behind me was the set of glass doors that led out to the balcony. I sat there frozen, still looking at the front door. I realized that the knock sounded funny because someone was knocking on the glass. I suddenly felt really afraid and turned to look at the doors. Standing at my balcony door was a boy. He was about twelve or thirteen years old.His face seemed pale and his eyes were solid black. He was knocking on the glass and staring at me. It scared the hell out of me. I ran to the bedroom and called building security. It only took a couple of minutes for the security guy to knock on the front door and announce himself. I didn't even look towards the glass doors again until I let the security officer in. He told me that he'd looked around outside and didn't see anyone around. I told him again what had happened, leaving out the part about the black eyes. He went out on the balcony and looked around. He seemed like he didn't believe me because he said no one could get down that fast and he had been on the ground level, right outside when I called. He assured me that everything was fine and that he'd look around again.

I've never been able to get the image of that kid out of my head. Those black eyes were so disturbing. Did he climb up to my third story balcony? Was he going to break in? How did he get down so quickly without the security guards seeing him? These questions and others have bothered me since that day. I didn't spend much time in that apartment after the incident, but I never saw the kid again. A few months ago, my sister told me about what are called the "black eyed kids" and I believe that's what I saw."

Was Sandra merely imagining things? Was she not as completely conscious as she thought she was, or was she so exhausted and stressed from work that it created a delusion? These would be common arguments from those anxious to discount BEK encounters. For her part, Sandra is convinced the child was a real, physical being. Furthermore, concern about the sighting caused her to consult a physician following the incident and she received a clean bill of health.

Sandra was never completely comfortable in the apartment after the encounter, and she tried to spend as little time there as possible until her contract was complete. She never slept on the couch again but only in her bed with the bedroom door locked.

Is It Food Time?

I've received a lot of accounts of black eyed children from the state of Texas and by far one of the creepiest accounts in my files comes from the Lone Star State. It's always interesting to find accounts of paranormal activity that include the reaction of an animal. Since they have a different level of perception than humans, it's beneficial to note how animals respond to various manifestations, whether in a positive or negative manner. It's well known that animals have detected earthquakes and other natural phenomena, perhaps their sensitivity can aid us in understanding the paranormal. I've only heard of a few encounters with black eyed beings wherein an animal has been present. The first account I received was from a man in Texas who encountered a black eyed kid in his yard. The man's pet pit bull quickly arrived on the scene and the results were stunning.

Chuck lives west of the Dallas, Texas metro area. He encountered a BEK in his front yard after returning from the supermarket early one evening in April 2012.

"I had run up to the store to get a few things that my wife asked for. I was only gone about a half an hour. I pulled my truck up into the driveway, got the two bags and headed for the front door. There wasn't anyone around, I'd swear. We have a small set of steps that go up to the front door. I had the two bags in one hand and I opened the front door with the other. We're pretty far out from the city and sometimes don't lock the doors if we're just running an errand. Just as I pushed the door open, I heard somebody speak to my right. It scared the hell out of me and I jerked my hand back from the door, just leaving it open.

There was this boy standing there. He wasn't up on the steps; he was beside them in the yard. I swear he must have come out of nowhere. He was wearing one of those hoodies with the hood pulled up. It was grey and he was wearing some jeans. The weird thing was what he said, he asked me:

"Is it food time?"

I mean, who asks a question like that? I didn't even know what to say, I just stood there trying to figure out who this kid was, I'd never seen him before and I knew all the folks around us. Then he spoke again:

"It's food time, you should invite me in."

I thought he was looking at the plastic bags I had and maybe saw the ribs I had in there, but it was such a strange question. I was thinking, this kid's not coming in my house. Just then, I heard my dog barking. I could hear him running through the house, towards the front door. My dog is a three-year-old pit bull that I raised from a pup.

He's well trained and he's never once not listened to my commands. He's a great guard dog, and he won't back down from anything or anyone. I've seen this dog kill a rattlesnake before.

I watched my dog turn the corner into the living room at a run. We've got wooden floors and it was like all of a sudden, the dog tried to put his brakes on. He slid across the floor to the door and almost fell over himself getting turned around. He went from full attack mode, to scared to death mode in a matter of seconds. He tucked his tail, put his head low and ran away whining. I'd never seen this dog whine like that in my life, and I'd never seen him act scared of anything. Seeing him act like that scared the hell out of me.

I looked back at that kid and he was looking up at me with a little smile. That's when I saw his eyes; they were solid black, no whites in that kid's eyes. Something about this creepy looking kid had scared my dog and now I was feeling scared myself. I got in the door as quick as I could and slammed it shut behind me. I went to the kitchen and put the bags down. I realized that I was shaking. I don't know what it was about that kid but it really shook me up. I went back to the front room and looked through the small slits of the blinds. I didn't see the kid anywhere. I opened the blinds a little more and could see the yard; there was no sign of him. I finally went back to the front door and had a look around the house but there was no sign of the boy with black eyes.

When I went back in the house, my wife wanted to know what was wrong with the dog because he was hiding under the bed. I tried for some time to get him out but all he would do was whine. I finally had to drag him out but he went right back under there.

The next several days and nights, that dog stayed mostly under the bed. He'd go outside when he needed to, but only through the back door."

Chuck reports it took a few weeks for his dog's behavior to return to normal. In a recent communication, he told me he felt his dog had never fully recovered from whatever frightened him. On a personal level, he feels haunted by the encounter with the strange black eyed boy. He has no explanation as to why he and his dog sensed such fear from just seeing or sensing a teenage boy.

Chuck estimates the kid was about fourteen years old. He soon asked his neighbors if they'd noticed any strangers in the area but no one had seen anything. Chuck's yard is open and clear. He's puzzled by the fact there was nothing for the child to hide behind near the door, as the nearest tree is at the front of the property. "There's nothing there" he reports, "not even a railing or anything at all to block my view of the front of the house as I walk to it." Yet somehow the boy just suddenly appeared.

Canines can of course sense fear in people and other animals. In this case the dog seems to have sensed the opposite, an impending danger from something that apparently terrified it. This reaction is especially curious when considering that many of those who encounter the black eyed children claim they felt as if they were being "looked over by a predator."

Chuck was unable to determine how close his dog got to the BEK before its fear reaction kicked in. "It all happened so quick" he states, "I know it must have been some time around the front door, because that's when I saw him (the dog) try to stop his run."

Perhaps the animal was acting appropriately in the face of something more powerful than it was. Despite the dog's training, it could not overcome the fear it experienced, and the overwhelming energy projected by the black eyed child.

The encounter is fascinating, and like many things paranormal, leaves more questions hanging in the air than it answers. I hope more encounters between BEK and animals will surface, offering up further insight from the animal kingdom to help determine the nature of these strange beings.

Black Eyed Spirit

I received an intriguing account of BEKs from Pittsburgh, Pennsylvania. While it is typical in many respects, there's at least one stark difference from most black eyed child encounters. The BEK does not seem to be completely physical in form. The child does not exhibit any feet, rather the body simply fades away at the lower part of the legs. This led the witness to believe he had encountered a ghost.

"My wife and I moved to Pittsburgh, PA in 2001. She had family in the area and she'd always wanted to be close to them. At first, we rented an apartment for a year while we settled into new jobs. Once the year was up and we had decided to stay in the area, we started looking for a house. By 2002, we moved into our own house, a one-story place that we found for a good price. The neighborhood was clean and quiet and within a couple of months, we had met most of the families on the block. It was a great place to live.

My wife and I both worked about the same hours, so except for occasional overtime, we usually arrived home around the same time. This strange incident happened to us in September of 2002. It was a weekday, around the latter part of the month. I got home first, and my wife about a half hour after me. We talked for a minute but my wife wasn't feeling too well, so she went to the bedroom to lay down. I was sitting in the living room, watching some sports. About fifteen minutes after my wife had gone to the bedroom; there was a knock at the front door. It was sort of loud and I didn't want it to wake her so I put my drink and the TV remote down and quickly got up. It was strange because the knocking just kept going, the person wouldn't let up.

When I opened the door, there was this kid standing on the step. He was wearing a gray hooded top and his hands were stuck in the pockets. I wondered for a moment how he had been knocking because his hands were in his pockets. I'd never seen this boy in the neighborhood before. He was staring straight at me and his look was rather mean. Before I even said anything, this kid says 'I want to come into your house now.' The hair on the back of my neck went up; this kid's tone was so cold. He looked about ten years old, and this didn't sound right coming from him. I looked at him and realized his eyes were solid black. I felt like I was starting to panic. I don't know why I did it, but I looked beyond him, out to the street. Maybe I was hoping there was someone else out there, I don't know. When I looked back at the boy, I only glanced at his face, I couldn't stand those eyes. Then I glanced down and realized I couldn't really see his feet. I know how strange this sounds. I don't really know how to explain it; it's almost like his legs just faded away. I slammed the door on him and turned around to see my wife rushing into the room. She looked frightened and said to me 'There's a kid knocking on the bedroom window and he has black eyes!' I was so stunned I didn't know what to say. I opened the front door again but there was no one there. I ran outside and went to the corner of the house where our bedroom windows were, again there was no one there. There must have been two of those kids, but I simply can't imagine that they were able to get away from the house so quickly. There was something so unnatural about the boy I saw standing on the steps, and I've never understood why I couldn't see his feet. For a long time, I thought that we had seen ghosts. It's only in the past year that we came across stories of the black eyed children on the Internet. We now believe this is what we witnessed. Thankfully, they never returned."

Perhaps this account offers a vital clue in terms of the BEKs and their seeming ability to come and go so quickly. If their true nature is something akin to a spirit, then they may be able to materialize at will. They do, after all, share many traits in common with apparitions. A malicious spirit taking physical form in order to cause trouble could fit the bill and explain black eyed kid encounters. That is, except for the other nagging aspects that are NOT akin to ghostly manifestations. As always, the more information we have, the more questions we have.

Omens of Death

Nothing positive ever seems to result from BEK encounters, but some of the most disturbing accounts of black eyed children are those that imply the kids are omens of death or misfortune. Some of those who encounter the kids under these conditions feel the children actually bring the bad luck and cast it on the victims, while others feel the children were somehow drawn to the negative experiences that were unfolding at the time.

Marcia from Ohio gave me her account detailing an encounter with a pair of black eyed boys in Virginia that occurred in the summer of 2011.

"My mother took very ill and had to go to the hospital. She was having heart problems to top it off, so they ended up keeping her at the hospital. Since my mom lived alone, my sister and I went to stay at her house in Virginia. It kept us close by and we could go to visit her during visiting hours. We could also watch her two cats and keep the house for her. My father had passed away two years before, and since that time my mom had really kept to herself. Her house was in a very quiet, safe neighborhood and she knew everyone around her.

On a Monday evening, we got back from the hospital, went into the house and decided to fix something to eat. I don't think either one of us was really hungry; we just wanted something to keep busy. The doctors had told us that our mom wasn't doing very well and that they weren't sure what else to do for her.

I was in the kitchen with my sister and we were talking when both of us looked up at each other. We both thought we had heard something. I asked my sister if she'd heard knocking and she said yes, that she had heard it too. We both walked into the living room and just then, we heard it again, someone was knocking on the front door. 'I wonder if the doorbell's broken,' I said out loud. We'd had several visitors; people were always stopping by who knew my mom, checking in to see if they could do anything, and to see if she was better.

I opened the door, just thinking it was another neighbor, but it wasn't. There were two kids standing at the door. They were about ten years old. I have kids myself that are the same age, so I was pretty sure of that. The boy on the right was looking at the ground, but the boy on the left looked straight at my sister and I as soon as the door opened. His eyes were solid black. They were so black that they were shiny. I didn't know what to say, I'd never seen anyone without any whites in their eyes. Soon as the door opened, that boy said, "You're going to invite us in." I slammed the door without even thinking about it. I was afraid they were some kind of gang members or something. Right after the door slammed, we heard a noise from right outside that I can only describe as a cat in pain. It was much louder than a cat would be though. We ran to the kitchen and I phoned the next-door neighbor who was a retired policeman. It only took him a minute to get to our house. He searched all over but couldn't find any sign of the two boys.

A short time later, we received a call from the hospital. Our mom had passed away. I don't know what the boys were but it scares me that they showed up at the time when my mom passed away. Those boys terrified me and even thinking about it now, almost a year later, it still frightens me."

Marcia's encounter stands out because her sister also witnessed the black eyed child. Most often, victims of the BEKs are alone. The strange cat-like sound the sisters heard outside is unusual but not completely unheard of. A case I documented from the 1950s included a BEK who, "screeched like a bobcat." The sisters remain convinced their sighting of the black eyed boys was a manifestation of death, a symbol of the passing of their mother. They are at a loss to understand why the incident occurred but they both hope never to see such children again.

Black Eyed Adults

One of the most common questions I have heard in relation to the black eyed children is not about the kids at all. I'm constantly asked "Are there any accounts of black eyed adults?" The short answer is yes, there are. Over the years, I've come across quite a number of weird encounters that involved adults with solid black eyes. While the number doesn't come close to BEK encounters, it's still enough to warrant a look. As you might imagine, the internet is rife with such tales, and while many of these may be fabrications, some of them may indeed be genuine encounters. Full sclera contact lenses are available from theatrical costume suppliers and online costume shops, and these could account for some of the black eyed adult sightings. I'm very doubtful that children are spending so much money on contact lenses for a quick thrill. Even discarding obvious hoaxes and pranks however, there are still some strange encounters that can't be easily dismissed.

Black eyed adult encounters, although smaller in number, do have similarities with standard BEK encounters. People report that the black eyed man or woman does not act in a normal fashion. Pale skin is usually noted, as is a monotone manner of speech and odd, unnatural statements or questions. Here are a couple of black eyed adult encounters I have received.

Black Eyes and Baguettes

A woman in Fairfax, Virginia, sent me a brief account of her encounter with a black eyed man in a grocery store. Kimberly recounts her story:

"I was out visiting my sister since we both had the day off. We planned on having dinner together at her house and we had gone to the store to get some items. We were walking around the store talking and trying to remember everything we needed. My sister suddenly remembered that we needed a baguette but we had already passed the bakery. I said, 'no problem, I'll run back and grab one; you keep getting the other things we need.' I went over to the bakery to get the bread. The store keeps fresh baguettes in a big basket at the end of one of their table displays. As I neared the basket, I noticed there was a man standing there. He was dressed in normal clothes, I don't really remember them much but I think they were grey or maybe brown.

What was weird though, was that he had a baguette in his hands and he was sliding it in and out of the bag. My first thought was that it was disgusting because he was putting his hands all over the bread. I stood and watched him for a moment. He would hold the bag in one hand and tip it to let the bread slide out. One loaf fell to the floor and he just looked down at it for a moment then let the bag fall from his hand too. Then he picked up another loaf and started doing the same thing. I wanted to say something but I didn't know what kind of creepy guy this was playing with bread. It was as if he didn't even know what it was or why it was in the bag.

I was thinking about all kinds of things. I didn't want to buy any bread because I didn't know how many loaves this guy had put his hands on. Then I thought, well, he must be strung out on something and he's just tripping, having some weird moment with the feel of the bread. As all of this was running through my mind, the man suddenly stopped, held the bread upright, and turned and looked directly at me. It was like he suddenly knew I was standing there watching him. It was totally creepy and I had the sudden feeling that he knew what I was thinking when I was staring at him. The worst part was, when he turned his head and stared back at me, I saw his eyes. They were solid black. I honestly didn't think such a thing was possible and it gave me a chill. I took a couple of steps back. I was right by the bakery counter and someone said, "Can I help you?" I turned and there was a woman behind the counter. I pointed over to the basket of French bread but didn't say anything. Her eyes followed my pointing finger, but as she was looking, I suddenly realized that the man was gone and was nowhere to be seen. The whole thing was even more disturbing at that point. The bakery section is pretty big and wide open. The displays are not tall and there were only a couple of other customers around. I simply don't believe he could have slipped off that quickly, but I have no idea how he vanished so suddenly. The loaf of bread was still on the floor where he had dropped it, along with the empty bag that he had tossed down. The woman behind the counter asked me what was wrong and I just made a quick apology, telling her there was a strange man who had dumped some bread on the floor. She thanked me for letting her know and said that someone would clean it up. I darted off to go find my sister. When she asked where the bread was, I just told her there wasn't any. I was very disturbed and wanted out of the store as quickly as possible. I kept looking around every aisle thinking I was going to see that weird man again. I was even paranoid when we walked out to the car. It wasn't until we were back at my sister's place that I finally told her the whole story. I still don't know what that man was or why he was doing that with the bread. He seemed confused at first, but when he looked at me, I had the worst feeling of dread."

Kimberly was a reliable witness; she works in an accounting office for the state and, according to her, her life is all about 'facts' and numbers. Her encounter left her puzzled and for a time she avoided returning to the grocery store where she had seen the black eyed man. Kimberly has a hard time believing in anything paranormal, but the feelings she experienced when confronted with the man have not been easy to forget.

"Any time I've thought about the incident, I've tried to tell myself it was just some weird guy on drugs, but what if it wasn't? Things about the whole incident just don't make sense and I can't ignore what I experienced. I just don't want to run into such a creepy character again."

It seems the black eyed man in the bakery was puzzled by a loaf of bread in a bag. Why would a normal person be so confused by what most of us consider a common, everyday item? This type of incident is in fact a common theme in accounts of both black eyed people and the infamous men in black. It would appear that something in their 'programming' is not up to speed, and they are perhaps unfamiliar with many normal, everyday items most of us take for granted.

Relax, You Didn't See Anything

Shannon is a professional massage therapist. She's worked in the field for seven years, and while she encounters the occasional 'creepy guy' most of her clients are normal, hard-working people trying to stay healthy. She reports that most of her clientele consists of athletes and business people, i.e., office workers. Nothing quite prepared her for a strange revelation about one of her regular clients.

"I had this client; he seemed to be a completely normal guy. He owned some kind of mortgage business and he told me that he was stressed a lot because of all the number crunching and all the work sitting at a desk. He set up to do a weekly massage with me. He was there every Thursday like clockwork, always on time. He never really wanted to talk much, which was fine with me. I always thought there was something a little off about him, but I couldn't put my finger on what it was. Anyway, he didn't hit on me or anything, which was nice. Massage is a difficult business and you get a few creeps here and there that think they're going to get something other than bodywork. I did a regular massage for this man, who called himself John, for almost two years. Then, one week, he missed his appointment. He didn't show up, didn't call, nothing. It had never happened with him before. I tried to call him early the following week to see if he intended to come in for his regular massage but I found that his phone was disconnected. I thought it was all kind of odd. Anyway, I didn't fill his slot, just by coincidence as no one called or wanted that particular hour. Then on Thursday, he showed up, right on time like normal for his appointment. I was surprised because I thought he must have moved or something. I made a comment about his work number being out of service but he just mumbled something that I couldn't understand, so I dropped the topic.

He got on the table and I started doing the massage. One thing I noticed was that he was rather cold to the touch. I had never really noticed that with him before. He turned over onto his back and I continued the massage. That's when things became weird. His cell phone, which was sitting on a table right in the office with us, started ringing. The volume was up pretty loud. When the cell phone rang, his eyes snapped open. They were solid black! I jerked my hands back and took a step away from him. He looked straight at me for a moment. The cell phone stopped ringing; he closed his eyes for a moment and let a loud breath out. Then he opened his eyes and they were more normal, still very dark, but I thought I could now see some whites where there weren't any before. He was sort of squinting so it was hard to tell. He said to me, "You didn't see anything, everything is fine." I'm thinking, no, everything is not fine. I started yelling at him to get out of my office. I turned my head away from him because I was so upset, I just kept saying, get out, get out. All the time he was talking in a monotone voice, telling me that everything was fine, that I should relax, that I didn't see what I thought I saw. I started to yell louder but it wasn't working. I left my office through the side door. I went and called my girlfriend who's also a massage therapist and had her come over.

When she got there, we both went into my office together and the guy was gone. When I started thinking about the whole thing, I realized that I couldn't remember ever seeing his eyes before that. He was one of those people who never wanted to make eye contact. Plus, when he came and left, he always wore those old mirrored sunglasses. He would keep his eyes shut the whole time he was on the table, so thinking back, it's as if he made an effort to never let me see his eyes."

Shannon is convinced she 'never' saw the man's eyes prior to the incident. This could be a result of her fear projecting more details into her encounter, or perhaps her memory is indeed accurate. It is odd that the gentleman made at least some effort to obscure his eyes on a regular basis. His curious reaction and his monotone speech in the aftermath harken back to classic black eyed kid encounters. Was he attempting to gain control of the situation, and Shannon's mind, in order to erase her memory of the incident? Shannon and her friend later looked up the man's business and could find no listing for it online or in phone books. Following up on the disconnected phone number, they found that the last owner of the number had been a pizza delivery service.

A Pair of Black Eyed Encounters

Sherry has had two very different encounters with black eyed people and both were unusual. Her first incident occurred in 1988 while she was living in Waterville, Maine. Sherry and her fourteen-year-old son were shopping at a grocery store when they saw a very strange toddler. Sherry recounts her experience:

"This was daytime, and warm weather for we didn't have coats on. In front of us was a toddler in a shopping cart facing us... His mom was talking to the cashier and unloading the cart on the counter. We both happened to look at this toddler at the same time, and his eyes were totally black...no white at all.... We were both so shocked and unnerved that we didn't even speak to each other.... I looked away to the right, and my son next to me looked away to the left... Then I looked back 'cuz I couldn't believe it. And his mom was talking to the cashier like nothing was wrong....but this creepy, scary toddler was staring straight at us. I looked away again.

After the mom paid and pushed the cart and kid out ...we moved up and whispered to each other 'What the Hell was that...? Did you see its eyes?' We checked out and kept talking about it on the way out... We never saw them outside or again. We both felt evil from this toddler and we were totally creeped out by it. The toddler was dressed normal and everything about it was normal except the eyes. It did not speak to us. I think on the way home we were numb 'cuz we couldn't figure it out. I tried to find something at the time online about it and couldn't."

Encountering such a young child with solid black eyes is unusual; most often, BEKs are estimated to be between the ages of ten to fourteen. This rates as the youngest black eyed child report I have received.

It's rare to find someone who has had more than one encounter with black eyed beings, but Sherry falls into this small group. Sherry had another black eyed person encounter years later of a very different nature. The next event occurred while she was working at the Harvest Time Health Food store in Augusta, Maine. Sherry was still residing in Waterville, Maine and commuted to work. This encounter was in early October in the mid-2000s. She reports:

"I was there early to open the store and I was the only one up at the cash register, I remember two old women coming in and going to the back of the store to shop. And then an old man showed up at the glass door, off to the side of the glass door, and looked in at me. He had solid black eyes. He never came in. I saw him and tried to tell myself he was just an old man with one of the old women shopping there. But I noticed him because he was staring in at me. Then I realized he was evil and I put up my white light protection. I then saw him stare at me a few more seconds and leave in a pickup truck. He had on a hat and plaid fall coat. He was not with the old women. I would guess his age around early 70's. Having that happen, you would think I would remember it all day...but I immediately forgot the incident for two days. This happened on a Wednesday. Then on Friday morning I woke up and remembered the whole thing. I started to shake and cry and got up,went in my son's room and woke him up... I told him what I remembered... He said, 'Jesus Mom; you are scaring the crap out of me'... I said, 'What do I do? He knows where I work.' He said, 'Well, if he knows where you work he most likely knows where you live too.' I was telling him this old man looked just like the toddler we had seen years ago. He said, 'Go smudge and do your prayers and try not to worry.' So, I did and I felt a little better. Never saw the old man with the black eyes ever again. But at the time, I was helping a lot of customers get well...and even helping them with alternative meds after hours. I was doing a good job and thought maybe I was standing out, as if the dark ones didn't like the good work I was doing. I couldn't think of anything else at the time.

I realized the old man made me forget what happened because I didn't put up protection fast enough... So yes, there must have been some kind of mind control going on. But when I first saw him, I was so shocked I tried to rationalize and make excuses he was with the old women. After the second look at him, I knew he was evil."

Sherry's background includes alternative healing. She is currently a Reiki master and shamanic practitioner, although at the time of her encounters she did not practice these arts. She considers herself a spiritual person with a strong belief in God. She believes the black eyed beings she encountered were demonic in nature. After each of her encounters, she had a difficult time moving past the experience. She says she worried for a time the black eyed beings would return. She still has many unanswered questions regarding what she encountered and she says she is disturbed to know "these things walk this earth."

A Black-Eyed Family?

For a long time reports of the black eyed children consistently came from people with no background or interest in the paranormal. With the increase in sightings, that is starting to change. A growing number of paranormal investigators, psychics and those interested in strange things are now having encounters with black eyed beings.

Christina George is a psychic and paranormal investigator on the west coast. Like many people in the field, she's encountered some strange things while investigating haunted sites and paranormal cases. Nothing however, really prepared her for her encounter with a set of black eyed people. Christina's account was originally posted on her website and titled "Black Eyed Kids Encounter...Or is it?" It is reprinted here with her permission:

"In the Summer of 2012, myself and a few members of my paranormal group had went up to see a client reporting being abducted, having an implant, as well as experiencing paranormal activity in the Redding, CA area. That area is known for UFO sightings as well as all kinds of strange activity. We got there and spent the whole day going thru medical paperwork as well as obtaining electronic readings and pics. We finished up our investigation where we all seemed to experience some kind of activity. I got home later that day and I had decided to go to the store with my roommate. Now before I go any further let me tell you this about my roommate so you can better comprehend what I am about to explain to you. I have been friends with him for over 20 years, he likes his privacy, and in fact our home is at the end of a dead end road that is backed up to a greenbelt, along with its own hill and creek down below, just outside my door. We do not answer our door to unannounced visits, and if he does answer it, he will let you know he is not happy about it. He also does not like when people are around our house since there is no reason to be on our property. So this is where the story gets weird.

We are driving back up to our home and standing on our grass in front of our house were 3 people. An older woman who was maybe 45, brown eyes, has a long hippy-like, made dress that was all wrinkled and some different colored sandals. Then there was a little African American girl, about 10yrs old, her hair was not combed... she had mismatched shorts and a t-shirt (also wrinkled), but she was very pale and almost looked sick and skinny and had a very dry and ashy appearance. And the third was a young boy, about 10yrs of age with a very blond, bowl cut hair with bangs straight across, and again mismatched shorts and shirt, but what really stood out was his pale white skin and piercing blue eyes.

So as we pull up and open our garage and park in front of it, my roommate says 'Who the hell are those people' I look but have no idea who these people are. I know just about every person in our subdivision, and I have never seen them. They were standing on our grass as if they were waiting for us. My roommate says I will be right back, I am going to find out why they are here and who they're looking for. I agreed and watched from the car as he walks over and starts talking to them, I am watching as he has his hand on his hips and then drops them to his side, he turns around walks back with no expression on his face, gets in the car and turns it back on and pulls into the garage and closes the door. I ask 'who were they? What did they want?' He replies in a very monotone voice 'They are looking for some feral kittens' which I found very strange since I have seen no kittens anywhere around the area. But what I found even more strange was the fact that he seemed to be ok with that answer and did not ask them to leave. I said 'why didn't you tell them to leave?' in which he replied 'it's ok, don't worry about it' and then exited the car, went into the house and went down into his room without saying another word to me.

I enter the house on the main floor and go upstairs but had a really weird feeling I could just not shake about what had just taken place so I went back down the stairs to the main floor of the house to the window I have next to my door and I peeked through the blinds to see if these people were really looking for kittens, or if they were even still outside. I look through the blinds and I see the woman standing on the side of the hill outside with one child on each side of her holding their hands, and as if they could sense that I was looking at them, they all three turned their heads and bodies around in perfect sync and looked dead at me. Now if that wasn't scary enough, I look and see that they all three now have completely black eyes with no whites visible at all. I remember it made their eyes look so big and scary. I was so terrified I jumped away from the blinds hitting my back on the door handle of the coat closet behind me hard. I looked again to make sure I wasn't imagining it only to see them still there staring. I screamed for my roommate and when he didn't come I ran downstairs to the lower level of the house and banged on his door yelling his name with no answer. I could hear what sounded like the shower going and I thought to myself how weird, why is he taking another shower. I run back upstairs not knowing what to do trying to calm myself down. I finally calm down and get the courage to go back to the blinds and peek through them, I now see that they have moved, they are near a tree standing in a circle holding hands, they are swaying back and forth and I can hear them saying what sounded almost like a chant. I hear and see them and at that moment again they all turn in unison and look directly at me, again seeing a closer look at them and they still have completely black eyes with no whites visible. Once again I get this overwhelming feeling of fear come over me. I run downstairs again and start banging on my roommates door with no response and now I have no idea what to do. I remember telling myself "come on Christina, you are a Paranormal Investigator people come to you because of stuff like this and you're never afraid, why are you so damn scared now. I somehow snap myself out of it and grab the doorknob, turn the handle and I yanked the door open forcefully walking out the door and looking right at them and saying 'Can I help you with something' they look over at me, drop their hands and the woman looks at me and says 'no, we're done' I was confused for a minute and I asked " did you find the kittens?" but they said nothing and walked off. I went in the house to try to get my roommate again and this time he is coming up the stairs as I am coming in and I yell to him 'come here, those people had black eyes,' they were holding hands and chanting, they knew I was looking at them along with many other things. He asked me where they were and I said come on they just walked away, we ran outside and down our walkway and they were gone. I even jumped in my car and drove around the subdivision because there is only one way in and one way out. But to my disappointment I found no one. It troubled me for a very long time.

I later spoke to my team and found that they were all reporting their own experiences of paranormal activity since returning from this client's house, but none like mine. I then contacted a good friend of mine Anthony Sanchez and told him about what had happened to me and he quickly told me he thought I had an encounter with what is called the Black Eyed Children. I was initially intrigued and started doing some research but quickly felt that maybe this wasn't what I experienced because of the differences in other reportings and mine. First they did not knock on my door and ask to come in, Second I saw the color of their eyes, which were originally brown and the little boy had blue and then they changed, and third, I couldn't find any reportings of them holding hands or chanting. I did feel a little defeated but knew nonetheless what I had experienced that day was real, but now I needed to figure out what this is, and what it means."

I met with Christina when I spoke for the Sacramento, California MUFON group in 2013. I found her account compelling because of the unusual elements, and because it fit the pattern of many accounts people had been sending me over the previous six months. In a follow-up post on her story, Christina wrote, in part:

"...went to the local Sacramento Mufon Meeting where the guest speaker David Weatherly who is the author of *Black Eyed Children* was going to be speaking on this phenomenon, so I thought it would be a great chance to ask some questions and possibly get some answers, and boy did I. After the meeting, I went over and spoke to David and found that what I had experienced has been reported to him on a few occasions but because it is kind of rare and I had seen the eyes change, he was very interested in my story and asked if he could include my story in his upcoming book. I of course, said yes as it was the least I could do; he didn't even realize how much his information helped me in getting the validations I needed. So now I know what it was, but now I am still faced with why? With being a paranormal investigator and a psychic I have seen and encountered paranormal phenomena throughout my whole life and I am left wondering why me?, but I guess that is what keeps me searching on this journey that is ever changing."

Christina echoes the question everyone who encounters these things asks. "Why me?" Despite all the accounts that have surfaced, nothing can really answer that question. I must admit, on some level it is good to see accounts surfacing from those with an interest in the paranormal. As more investigators seek answers, more answers may be forthcoming. As the overall number of encounters grows, so too do the details, with countless small bits of information; perhaps a clearer picture will emerge to tell us what exactly these beings are after, and where they are coming from. Until then we must contemplate the possibilities and wonder what lies on the other side when we hear a knock at the door.

Listening to so many accounts of black eyed beings over the years, there's a sense that something very strange is unfolding. As the number of encounters grow, the message that many witnesses derive from their encounters evolves. John, a man who has encountered both a BEK and a black eyed adult, believes we're seeing the unfolding of some sinister plan:

"I believe that, whatever these things are, they've been here all along, around us even though we haven't known about it. I just don't think they care as much about hiding anymore. That makes me very, very nervous because it feels like they're moving forward with their intent at a much quicker pace. I don't know what exactly that intent is, but I'll bet there's nothing good about it. My two encounters were disturbing and I'm even more concerned about what's in store for all of us if these things decide they want their presence known on a large scale. Laugh all you want, but the world is changing and I believe that these beings are going to continue to be a bigger part of it."

Truth is often much stranger than fiction, and the reality of these black eyed beings may prove to be something far more disturbing then we can imagine, or are prepared for.

Chapter Eight
Stealing the Breath of Life

Night Hags and Psychic Vampires

"Now I lay me down to sleep,

I pray the Lord my soul to keep.

If I should die before I wake,

I pray the Lord my soul to take."

This popular Christian prayer dates back to the medieval period. While many people have recited it through the years, few have taken note of its origins. The prayer is a reflection of early days when night, and the darkness, represented a time of fear and potential threat from the demonic forces that ever lurked just beyond the edge of our sight. Night was the time of devils and witches, succubi and vampires, demons and hags. It was a frightful period only passed through safely with the proper amount of prayer and the living of a faithful, righteous life.

Night attacks are an age-old phenomenon. From classical vampire lore depicting a dreaded bloodsucker creeping into bedchambers, to the vicious night hag who rides her victims to exhaustion, these terrors have long been a part of folklore. But are they merely tall tales and misunderstood medical conditions, or is there something more to the mystery?

Early occultist Dion Fortune wrote about psychic attack in her classic book, *"Psychic Self-Defense"* in 1930. Fortune believed her employer had attacked her psychically. Her energy was depleted and she was left so weak and vulnerable that she suffered a nervous breakdown. Fortune even reported finding dried blood on her pillow

141

and a small puncture mark on her jaw. She believed this was a physical manifestation of the psychic attack she had suffered. Fortune believed psychic attacks could come from physical, living people who were capable of astral travel and projecting their energy towards their intended victim. In this manner, the attacker could drain the victim of vital life force while they slept. Such attacks could be instigated by the practice of magic, giving the attacker the ability to drain life force from victims during waking hours as well.

Fortune also asserted non-physical entities could carry out psychic attacks. These beings were thought forms, demons or negative entities loosed upon the world. These creatures sought the energy of the living in order to continue their own existence. Throughout history, there are tales of such beings who live by stealing energy from other living creatures. Vampiric entities turn up in almost every culture around the world. The western world is most familiar with the iconic version of vampires —Count Dracula types who haunt the night, bite the necks of their victims and then return to sleep in a coffin when the sun arises. While this classical vampire myth has spread far and wide, not all creatures who live on energy fit the same mold as the European vampire. Other versions speak of creatures who steal the very life force on an energetic level.

Modern medicine dismisses the idea that entities are involved in night attacks. Some people believe the experiences are intense dreams and the victims are having recall of a dream or nightmare experience. Most doctors believe sleep paralysis is to blame for the hallucinations and terrors that people report. The images that patients recall, say doctors, are merely derived from cultural memory, folk tales, and early religious fears impressed upon them as children.

Despite medical advances and greater understanding of conditions like sleep paralysis, people around the world still experience terrible night attacks. Victims often awaken in the night, unable to move, with a feeling that someone, or something, is in their bedroom. In modern times, the phenomenon of alien abduction fits many of the same patterns, but not everyone is seeing little gray aliens during these terrifying encounters.

The night hag is still a prominent figure in night terrors. In classical tales, she is depicted as an old woman with wild, tangled hair, large eyes, rotting teeth and long, sharp fingernails. Victims of the hag wake in the night and find themselves immobilized. While they are able to open their eyes and hear sounds, they cannot move their bodies. The sense of evil is overwhelming and something is felt in the room, moving around them. The most dreadful aspect however, is the heavy weight the victim feels on their chest. And there, the image of a hideous old woman, slowly draining their energy, their very life force from them. Many cultures believe the old hag is a witch, out stealing energy to continue her dark works. Some literature connects her to the demonic 'Mara' from which the term nightmare is derived. This demon thrives on attacking people in the night when they are dreaming.

The Succubus

The succubus has been known since ancient times. They are dark beings who live in a spirit world and crave the energy and life essence of the living. The term "succubus" is derived from a Latin word meaning "to lie under." It is a demonic creature, female in form, that attacks men in the night. Their favorite time to attack is when their victim lies between the boundaries of sleep and waking consciousness. They can take the form of a beautiful woman, a person the victim knows or fantasizes about, or a completely unknown figure that radiates physical qualities the victim finds ideal. They favor men who sleep alone, or men who are having troubles with relationships; exploiting the weakness of their victim's insecurity. They will engage their victim in sexual intercourse as the route to steal his energy. The man will believe he is having a dream experience and will succumb to the guidance of the spirit woman. Once their victim is entranced, the succubus will return again and again, night after night, using their vampiric ability to drain energy on each visit. The victim will become weaker after each subsequent encounter with the succubus. Losing his vitality he will turn pale, experience a constant state of exhaustion, and feel unengaged in life. His weakening energy will often cause sickness, or at the very least extended periods of sleep, all of which make it easier for the succubus to drain energy quicker and quicker. A succubus will continue draining her victim until there is nothing left, leading to, in worst cases, death.

There is a male version of this dark being, referred to as an incubus, from the Latin term meaning, "to lie upon." The incubus uses the same techniques as the succubus when attacking its female victims. The plural terms for these entities are succubi and incubi.

During the infamous European witch-hunts, succubi and incubi were common topics during trials of witches. Church officials would often assert that witches were consorting with these sexual demons and agents of the devil. Witch hunters asserted that women were more vulnerable to demonic influence, and the devil took advantage of this by sending incubi to potential witches. These beings would seduce women in the night and trick them into signing pacts with the devil. Cases involving incubi were more commonly reported during this period, and so-called 'witch hunters' spent a great deal of time looking for evidence of such sexual relations. Agents of the inquisition also attempted to coerce confessions of such affairs from those they believed to be witches. As is well known, this was often done by methods of torture. Many church officials and demonologists of the period were quite focused on sexual acts and their connection to the devil. They asserted that Eve was to blame for original sin, and mankind's expulsion from the Garden of Eden; hence women must be in league with the devil and his minions. According to the text used by the inquisitors, the *"Malleus Maleficarum"* or the *"Hammer of the Witches,"* women who practiced witchcraft would willingly engage in relations with incubi, using the sexual act to further their connection to Satan. It's likely the repression of sexuality in the medieval church spurred those searching for witches to act out their sexual fantasies via hearing 'confessions' of perverted sexual activity.

Men were not free from the night demons during this period. According to the church, the devil could just as easily send a succubus to harass a man in the night. Sometimes Satan's agents, the witches, would summon a succubus or even align themselves with one to get at specific men. At times, men who accused women of witchcraft would claim the so-called witch herself had come to him in his dreams; seducing him in his sleep or waking him and using magic to force him to have intercourse. In this form, the witches would make promises and offers of power. Many such cases were likely the result of a man having his advances rejected, and in anger seek out revenge on the woman who spurned him. It was far too easy to accuse someone of witchcraft during the persecutions. Inquisitors thought if a succubus attacked a man, it was probably because he was pious and the devil wanted to tempt him away from the worship of the lord. Such trickery was, after all, the hallmark of Satan. If a witch or succubus could cause a man to have erotic dreams and nocturnal emissions, then she could steal his life force and the very energy of his existence.

While all of this could be dismissed and blamed on the crazed actions of the inquisitors, we must remember the origins of the succubus legend lie much further back in history. While the term succubus does not first appear until 1387, tales of creatures who attacked in the night and drained life force are much older. The connection between the succubus and the church has firmly placed even many modern versions squarely in the box of religiously defined parameters.

Lilith, the first Succubus

Hebrew tradition from the Middle Ages states that Adam's first wife, Lilith, was the original succubus. Lilith is not well known outside of Hebrew tradition, but she is a major figure in Hebrew myth and demonology, with roots reaching back through antiquity to Babylon and Sumer. Today she is still feared in some areas of the world.

Jewish literature developed an interpretive system called the *Midrash* as a supplement to glean deeper meaning from scripture. Information about Lilith can be found in Midrashim literature as well as in writings on the Kabbalah, the Jewish mystical system.

According to the texts, Lilith was outraged by the idea of submitting to her husband, Adam, and demanded she be treated as his equal. Lilith felt she should not have to lie beneath Adam during sexual intercourse. The results of her refusal were documented by Kabbalistic writer, Moses de Leon (1240-1305), in his thirteenth century text, the *"Sefer ha-Zohar:"*

"At the same time Jehovah created Adam, he created a woman, Lilith, who like Adam, was taken from the earth. She was given to Adam as his wife. But there was a dispute between them about a matter that when it came before the judges had to be discussed behind closed doors. She spoke the unspeakable name of Jehovah and vanished."

God sent three angels to Lilith in an attempt to bring her back to Adam. Despite their threats and her exile, she refused them saying she would henceforth do great harm and bring death to infants. She did vow however, to bypass anyone wearing an amulet bearing the names of the three angels who had come to her with the offer of redemption.

Lilith is only found once in the Old Testament, in Isaiah 34:14: "There shall the beasts of the desert meet with the jackals, and the wild goat shall cry to his fellow' the lilith also shall settle there, and find for herself a place of rest." The word lilith in this passage is sometimes translated as "night creature," or "screech owl," both terms associated with Lilith.

It is said Lilith flew off to the wastelands of the deserts near the red sea. She became the bride of the fallen angel Samael or Lucifer, the devil himself by some accounts. It seems the legend of Lilith merged with accounts from early Sumerian and Babylonian mythologies. She becomes a winged demon, still female in form, but now a vicious, harmful spirit that kills infants and plagues women when they are giving birth. She could now create nightmares, loss of sleep and general weakness to pregnant women. At her worst, she would cause miscarriages and infant deaths.

The Talmud describes her as a night demon with long hair, human in form but having wings with which to fly. In some guises, Lilith would take the form of a young, beautiful woman and seduce men. She would travel the world at night; angry and vengeful, she would go to men in their sleep, seduce them and drain them of their energy. Through these unions, countless children were created, demonic offspring she spread far and wide. These beings in turn became the succubi and incubi that would go on to plague the world. Other legends claim that Lilith through her union with Satan created a hundred children a day. A Muslim version of the story says the union of Lilith and Satan is what brought about the existence of the djinn.

After leaving Eden, she became associated with the night and her power was reputed to be stronger in the darkness. She is powerful during the full moon but is even stronger during the new moon, or the dark moon. She is associated with doorways and wells, both of which are places where she hides in wait for lone men she can seduce. The Hebrews called her the "demon of screeching" and she has been closely linked with wild animals, specifically the screech owl, the form of which she is able to assume. Lilith's role as the wife or lover of Satan was a particular focus during the witch-hunts of the medieval period in Europe. The church frequently named her the queen of the witches and it was thought women practicing the dark arts served her.

In some cases, Lilith is worshipped as a goddess, a version of the moon goddess, or as another version of the pagan 'great mother' goddess. This view was promoted by writer Gerald Gardner and later Doreen Valiente, both early pioneers of the modern 'Wicca' movement. This idea was popular in part because of its rejection of any traditional Christian concepts and its embrace of the erotic as a natural part of life.

Despite these isolated magical practitioners, most people still view Lilith as a negative entity, the first succubus and the driving force that created the legions of night creatures that haunt the dreams of many people. Through the ages, humans have sought methods to protect themselves from these demonic beings. The most popular has long been an amulet bearing the names of the three angels Lilith made her vow to: Senoy, Sansenoy and Semangelof. In early times such amulets would be hung on the cribs of newborns, placed in the corners of the room and worn by nursing mothers. Some even went so far as to draw a protective circle on the floor around the newborn's bed. Within the circle would be written the names of the three angels along with drawings to depict them.

Monks of the Middle Ages attempted to protect themselves from night invasions by sleeping with their hands crossed over their genitals and holding a crucifix. Various prayers are purported to work as protection against Lilith. Wearing holy symbols or hanging them from a bedpost is also a protective measure taken by many fearful of an encounter with Lilith.

Dark Attacks

The focus of both the succubus and incubus is to drain the energy and life force of their victims. It is purported that both of these entities could be summoned through the use of black magic, but just as often they would be drawn to their victims due to an 'opening' or vulnerability within the person. Church faithful would claim this was due to a weakness in the person's faith. More modern thinkers claim the entity is drawn near due to a weakness in the victim's energy field.

Some texts claim the succubus and incubus are actually one in the same, a demonic entity with the ability to switch gender depending on the targeted victim. This belief seems to have waned over the years, the two entities becoming viewed as separate manifestations of the same demonic group. While both the female and male versions of these creatures are similar in their goals and abilities, there are a few differences. Incubi are reputed to take great pleasure in degrading and perverting their female victims. They have a propensity to torment, creating terror and jealousy within the victim. Often they whisper instructions into the woman's ear, sometimes while she is asleep, attempting to program the listener to commit sins and cause destruction to their loved ones. Just as often they will whisper false information, causing the woman to become paranoid and fearful. The misshapen form of the incubi would often cause its victim pain during their sexual relations. Incubi take great pleasure in causing such discomfort. Their abusive nature and violent behavior is a hallmark of their manifestations.

The succubus was a bit more subtle in her actions, taking measures to manifest as the exact image her male victim found most appealing. The actual relations with this creature, however, are reported to be far from pleasant experiences. Some said that when engaging with a succubus, the act itself was painful and akin to penetrating a cavern of ice. Despite this less than pleasurable experience, the victim would fall to the creature's seduction night after night, suffering under the delusion he was with the woman of his dreams. The more engaged the man was with this idea, the greater the amount of energy drained in the liaisons. Men with particularly strong constitutions have always been especially prized by these energy-sucking creatures.

The succubus controls how much energy she takes and how quickly she takes it from her victim. While the rapid loss of life force would often lead to death, the succubus often had another goal — pregnancy. Classical studies on the succubus claim the demonic creatures could actually become pregnant by their male victims. The resulting hybrid child would be especially powerful, as it was part human and part demon. In the demonic realms such beings were highly regarded because of the ability to carry the energy of earth and hell at the same time, as well as having easy access to the earth realm. Such beings had no restriction on their travel between the realms and could create more darkness on earth, the ultimate goal of the demonic forces.

Light Defense

Both the succubus and incubus were usually invisible to everyone except their victims. On occasion, if someone entered the room while the victim was engaged with one of these entities, they may witness a shadowy form, or even on some occasions, the actual form the succubus/incubus was projecting. This made defense against the entities difficult, because often the victim would be quite weakened before anyone realized what was happening. Someone who had suffered multiple attacks by such a demonic entity required the assistance of a priest who could break the connection and banish the creature to the netherworld. In extreme cases, the rite of exorcism would be used to dispel a succubus or incubus, as many believed the creatures could 'take refuge' in the body of their victims.

Holy water was purported to be a powerful defense against these night intruders as was the reciting of the Ave Maria. The sign of the cross would expel them, as would the Lord's Prayer when spoken aloud. Modern spiritual practitioners who are not Christian, but believe in such energy thieves, say any spiritual symbol will assist in banishing them. Items that purify an environment, such as burning sage, frankincense and white candles are also effective. Light is considered a defense in some cases since dark entities like the succubus/incubus depend on the darkness to help mask their actions. People are also often safe from such encounters if they sleep in a room with other people, as the creatures do not like their activities to be observed.

College Fantasy Turned Nightmare

Modern accounts of succubus are not as rare as one might believe. Brandon's case falls squarely into the classical framework of succubus attacks. He was not raised Christian, so when his doctor's treatment failed to help him resolve the issue, he turned to a psychic:

"I started having dreams about a woman I had known almost seven years ago in college. I was always very, very attracted to her but at the same time, I never believed that she would be interested in me. We came from very different worlds and had different interests. She was dating a football player at the time and I honestly never considered even trying to ask her out. Anyway, the dreams at first were simple. I would run into her somewhere and we would start talking or maybe we would grab a bite to eat together. The dreams became more intense and soon they were outright sexual. I hadn't had such sexual dreams since I was a teenager. At this time, I was working for a financial firm and I put in long hours, trying to move up the corporate ladder. I started to feel exhausted all the time. I found that I was drinking several cups of coffee in the morning to get going. It got worse and I started drinking coffee all day just to keep up. One evening when I got home from work, I fell asleep in a chair in the living room. I must have dozed off almost right when I sat down because falling into the chair was about all I remembered. I had another dream about the woman; we were making love on the chair in my living room. I woke up with a sudden jolt; someone was pounding on the front door. I went to the door and it was a neighbor who came to get me because my car alarm was going off. He made a comment about how terrible I looked and that I should see a doctor. I told him I was fine, just tired. I cut the car alarm off and went back inside. Going to the bathroom, I took a look in the mirror and suddenly knew what my neighbor was talking about. My face was pale and I had large dark circles around my eyes, like I had been punched. I was sweating so much that my hair was wet. I had a very sunken look and it made me realize I hadn't eaten dinner. In fact, I suddenly thought about the fact that I had been eating very little."

Brandon reports that he went to a doctor and after an extensive checkup was told that his adrenals were in terrible condition. His doctor questioned him repeatedly to find out if Brandon was using any kind of illegal substance. He was not. He further informed his doctor of some of the strange things that had been happening to him in the night.

"I had started waking up from the dreams, positive that someone was in my room. At first, the feeling would be that the woman I dreamed of was there with me. When I became fully awake, my logical mind told me that was not the case and then I would feel that something creepy was in the room. The doctor insisted that I was suffering from sleep paralysis. He suggested some treatment, but honestly it didn't do me much good."

Concern for his health and continued deterioration drove Brandon to contact an alternative healer who could give him a spiritual approach.

"This woman knew exactly what was going on before I even told her the whole problem. She gave me a number of things to do to clear up the problem. With her help, I took care of cleansing my living space and banishing whatever was in there. The thing that puzzled me though was that she said there was a spirit of someone who had died involved in my situation. She said that I needed to understand that the person had passed on and that once I did, I would be ensured that the night attacker would never come back.

About three weeks after, I was starting to feel a little more like my old self. Then I awoke one night suddenly and the feeling was back. It was fleeting, but I was concerned. I got up very early that day and went to sit at a local coffee shop to do some work on my laptop. I was surprised to run into an old friend from college that I hadn't seen in years. We ended up sitting and talking over coffee for a couple of hours. At one point, he brought up the girl that I had crushed on in college. "That was tragic wasn't it?" he asked. I told him I didn't know what he was talking about at which he told me the story. The woman I had been so enamored with had died tragically in a drunk driving accident."

Brandon was stunned by the revelation but all the pieces had fallen together to help him understand what the psychic had told him. Was his attacker actually the woman he had adored in college? That's highly unlikely, but something chose to take her form and attempt to drain him of his life energy. After learning of the girl's death, Brandon made a point of visiting her grave and paying his last respects. Doing so, he believed, made him realize it was not her coming to him in the night, and he would never see her in life again. He has had no more night visitors and has moved on with his life.

Drained in Delhi

The succubus is not strictly a European phenomenon, such creatures can be found all over the world. This account was given to me by a man from India named Samir:

"This happened when I still lived in India. I was seventeen at the time and my brother was nineteen. We were both still living with our parents and we shared a bedroom. It was summer and very, very hot. We slept with the windows open because we needed the night breeze when it came. I did not sleep well very often because the heat made me restless. My brother slept well though. Then he started acting very odd and each day he seemed to be more and more tired. He said that he was sleeping but having strange dreams. No one knew what was wrong with him and this went on for about three weeks. One night I woke up to a strong wind coming in the window. The air felt good and I laid there listening to the night sounds. We lived in Delhi and there was always noise. I had a feeling that I cannot explain and I looked over at the window. I saw something that looked like a person; it had the form of a person, but it was all black like a shadow. I felt a very bad chill at seeing this thing. I watched as it moved over the windowsill; it moved like a snake, crawling from outside, over the bottom of the window and onto the floor. I kept trying to see details, to see a face or something, but there was nothing but darkness. I pinched my own arm very hard, just to make sure I was seeing this thing and to know that I was not dreaming. It moved across the room

151

with a strange motion, staying low on the floor like it was sliding on its belly. It went to my brother's bed and slid up the end then going all the way up until it was over him. It laid on top of him. I knew that I wasn't dreaming but I could not understand what this thing was. I had watched this creature come from outside and move across the room, all while I stayed completely still. Now, I knew that it was some kind of spirit and I was frightened but when it went on my brother, I bolted up in bed and started calling his name loudly. That thing turned and looked towards me and I could feel that it was angry. When it looked in my direction like that, I saw the face of a woman. I jumped from the bed and turned the light on, just as I turned, I could see it going back out of the window with that same strange movement. I woke my brother up, he was very groggy and it took a few moments. Our father came in and asked what all the shouting was about. I told him what I had seen and his face became very pale. He said he now understood what was wrong and that the thing I saw was stealing life force, *prana*. Early the next day, we sought out a holy man to help us. My brother recovered quickly and the thing I saw never came back. I know that it is still out there and that it preys on other people and this is what disturbs me. For a long time, I had trouble sleeping because I was afraid that she would return and perhaps attack me if I was asleep."

Stealing the Breath of Life

The Qarinah, of Arabic lore, is a succubus-like creature that drains the energy of its victims while they are dreaming. Legend says they can be perceived by those blessed with second sight or psychic vision. The Qarinah is known for taking the form of common household animals such as dogs and cats in order to gain entrance into homes and avoid detection.

In India, the Mohini is a succubus dressed in a white sari with long flowing hair. She is said to be a vengeful ghost, the spirit of a woman who died at the hands of a man. She seeks revenge by tempting men in the night and draining their energy, often lying in wait on lonely byways and at crossroads. Most of Asia has legends of vengeful, female spirits who behave in a similar manner. Usually, they are perceived as a literal spirit of the deceased rather than a demonic creature like the European version of the succubus. The results of encounters with them can be very similar, but with a loss of life force and energy, and ultimately, death.

China has a unique version of an energy vampire called the Jiang-Shi. While the creature is considered a part of myth and folklore, superstitions still run strong about it in parts of China. While traveling through China, I found some modern practitioners of the art of Feng Shui still take precautions against the Jiang-Shi. Feng Shui theory teaches that placing a six-inch piece of wood at thresholds along the width of doors will prevent these walking corpses and other evil beings from entering a building.

The term "Jiang-Shi" roughly translates as "stiff corpse" or "hopping corpse." The strange designation comes from a practice from China's early years. In the past, families who could not afford to travel to a distant location where a relative had died, would hire a Taoist magician to perform a ritual to retrieve the body. The magician would animate the corpse so it could travel back home itself. Since rigor mortis had often set in by the time the ritual was performed, the stiff corpse would often move with a hopping motion. Many precautions had to be taken during such operations to ensure that the corpse did not receive too much energy, lest it break free and begin to torment the living.

Chinese mysticism concepts teach that each individual has both a higher soul and a lower soul. When a person dies, it is the higher soul that moves on to the afterlife, crossing to the world beyond to join their ancestors. The lower soul however, remains with the corpse. This lower soul, desperate to cling to some semblance of life, would attempt to take any energy in the vicinity so the body could once again rise up.

The Jiang-Shi could be created due to an improper burial. Numerous things could cause a deceased person's body to become animated. The list included exposure to sunlight or direct moonlight, or an animal, particularly a cat jumping over or getting too close to the body. These things caused an energetic reaction in the corpse, causing it to rise up and seek more energy. Once animated such beings had one purpose, to steal the breath of the living.

It is interesting to note that in Chinese, the word "qi," westernized as "chi," translates as both breath and energy. This breath of life was the vital energy these animated corpses desperately sought.

One popular story still told in China concerns a group of travelers who couldn't find a place to rest. Out of options, an innkeeper informs them that he does have a room, but that it contains the corpse of his daughter-in-law who just passed away. Out of choices, and too exhausted to continue their journey, the travelers decide to take the accommodations. The corpse lies behind a curtain in the room. Trying to ignore its presence, the travelers settle in for the night. Since they are so tired, they are soon fast asleep. One of them wakes up however, disturbed by the loud snoring of his companions. Opening his eyes, he sees the figure of a pale girl drawing back the curtains and moving towards the sleeping men. One by one, she stands over the men. She leans in close, and each time, the man's snoring stops. Suddenly, the girl hears the frightened man and looks at him. He runs from the room and she pursues him. The man falls at the base of a tree and passes out. The next morning, the man wakes to find the stiff corpse still standing over him, her long fingernails buried in the bark of the tree. She had dug them in so deep she became trapped. Villagers came and cut the corpse loose, promptly burying her so she would not trouble anyone else. The other three travelers were found dead in the inn, all their life energy drained.

The Jiang-Shi is not a being with a conscious, driving desire to seek out victims. Rather, it reacts to the simple need for energy. This drives it to seek the living. Traditionally, the creatures were said to be blind and only tracked their prey by the sound of their breathing. For this reason, it was believed that holding the breath when in the presence of a Jiang-Shi was a defense against the creature. While many depictions of the creature showed them as normal humans with a sunken appearance, other accounts say their eyes glowed red due to the lack of a higher soul. It is also believed that the Jiang-Shi would develop long talons in order to help it capture living prey.

Numerous protections were devised against these creatures. Basic defenses included loud noises, especially those that replicated thunder, one of the Jiang-Shi's vulnerabilities. Iron filings were especially prized as they were reputed to create a barrier that the creatures could not penetrate. If one of these walking corpses was spotted, a Taoist priest was usually called in to deal with the situation. The priest would perform a ritual, and activate talismans written on rice paper with red ink or even blood. Once empowered, the talisman could be applied to the forehead of a Jiang-Shi, causing it to fall under a spell. Villagers could then bury the body before it became free. Unlike such creatures in the West, once buried, the Jiang-Shi could not rise again.

Chinese occultism and magic are not very well known in the West, but the traditions are rich and diverse. In some darker aspects of the magical arts, there are methods taught to steal the energy of other living creatures. The chi, or life force, is seen as the prize to those who practice these dark arts and such techniques may be one of the roots of the Jiang-Shi legend. I spoke to Emily, a Chinese-American woman who has spent a lot of time studying the traditional lore of her family's country. She agrees with this possibility, stating:

"Some of the darker magics were taught a long time ago. Some of the magical sects were at odds with each other and would devise ways to attack each other; it was especially valuable to devise attacks that were not direct. I also suspect that after contact with the West, the idea of the European vampire was blended in to the mix and some of these dark practitioners may have thought it would be a good idea to try to create such beings to attack their rivals. Really, the lore of the Jiang-Shi borrows elements of the European vampire and the African zombie, but the whole motivation is rooted in stealing the chi of others. That is very Asian in its thinking."

Energy Thieves

In every crowd it seems, there are people who are difficult to be around. They are generally depressed and down, living in a state of sadness on a daily basis. It's dreadful to be in their presence, because inevitably, you leave feeling depressed and sad yourself. American author Albert Bernstein dubbed such people "emotional vampires." They are people with personality disorders who drain emotional energy from those around them.

These people are, usually inadvertently, a type of psychic vampire. They live and thrive by "feeding" off the life force and energy of other people. Just being near them leads to exhaustion, headaches, depression and sadness. Occultist Dion Fortune believed psychic vampirism was a combination of psychic and psychological pathology, asserting that some mental conditions could lead to a propensity to drain others of energy through psychic means.

While Fortune wrote about such topics extensively in the 1930s, the term found new life much later, in the 1960s, when it was popularized by the self-proclaimed head of the Church of Satan, Anton LaVey. LaVey, showman that he was, claimed to have coined the term himself when he wrote about it in the Satanic Bible. LaVey saw psychic vampires as a form of parasite, weak on an emotional and spiritual level; living like leeches, draining vital energy from those around them. He also believed some people could have energetic or spiritual attachments that were responsible for this behavior.

In modern times, the rise of the "vampire subculture" has seen the inclusion of psychic vampires as an aspect of their beliefs. These are people who believe they are vampires, actively practicing the art of taking energy from other people though psychic means. Within the vampire circles, the act is considered intimate and is only done with the mutual consent of both parties. These "psi-vamps" as they are sometimes called, believe they need to draw energy from other living beings in order to continue thriving themselves, and to keep their spiritual energies in balance.

But perhaps there are other beings out there who do not care about consent or agreement, people who are quite conscious of their need for the energy of others and who take great pleasure in stealing it whenever the opportunity arises. There have been some reports that have come across my desk that imply just such a possibility. Take the case of Dinah.

Dinah encountered a woman she believes was not quite human. The encounter took place in a busy New York City nightclub and the events still haunt her to this day. She recounts her story:

"So I will start by saying that as far as I can remember I have always been sensitive. I have become comfortable with that and whenever something out of the ordinary happens, I deal with it and move on. On this evening, I went to N.Y.C to see a friend who was working at a lounge called Faluka in the Village. He is a D.J. and had a regular party there every Tuesday night. The place has a Persian, Middle Eastern feel and you can relax with a drink or smoke a hookah. I arrived, said hello to the people I knew, and was introduced to some new people, one of them being this Asian woman and her boyfriend. I believe she was from Japan, because she had mentioned that she wanted the D.J. to go to Japan for a visit. Anyway, as the night progressed she made some comments about how pretty I was, and the strange thing about it was that she kept touching my face. Like she was examining me...she would grab my chin and every time she did her sharp finger nails would kind of poke me. Now this is New York and I don't know about other places, but I would never touch someone's face unless I was intimate or very good friends with them. I just took it as she being Asian, and they have different customs.

Moving forward I started to feel uncomfortable, because she kept being in my personal space and there was something strange about her. Meanwhile her boyfriend never said anything; he just watched. I made my way to the dance floor, which is not very big and started to dance and enjoy the music. Now, I realized a few years back that sometimes when I dance I pray. I also feel my energy grow and I have had people ask if they can touch me because they said they could see my aura... I don't know if that's true, but it has happened more than once. Anyway, going back to that evening, I was on the dance floor and here comes the woman and her boyfriend and she starts trying to dance with me and be in my face. At this time, I'm starting to get annoyed so I casually turn my back on her as we are dancing. That's when she grabbed me by the waist and turned me around as if I was a feather. I'm not a big girl, but I'm very sure-footed and strong. She was a petite person also, and it was as though I didn't weigh anything. That's when it felt like she had punched me in the stomach, but in reverse and I bent over grabbing my stomach. It felt like she sucked all my energy right out of my body thru my groin and stomach area. Then when I looked up at her, she snickered and her face morphed.... Half her face changed and her eyes flickered. They changed shape and color... Hard to explain. I then just looked at her with what I'm sure was pure horror on my face, and that's when she said to her boyfriend, "She can see." So now, I run upstairs to the DJ booth, which is located in a small loft area above the dance floor. I tried to tell my friends what had happened, and I think they thought I had been drinking or something, but I don't drink. Not five minutes later, the woman and her boyfriend come up the ladder and sit in the D.J booth area. I feel liked a trapped animal and I had to pass right by her to get down. That's when my girlfriend, who I had told what had happened, made eye contact with me. So I felt like I could pass by them safely. When I did try to pass the Asian reached out to touch me, and I said to her very sternly, "Dont F*&%ing Touch Me!"

That's when she just laughed and smiled. Well, when my friend saw her reaction, she realized something was wrong and started to believe me... I left the lounge and have never been back since. Now my first impression of what she is, is DEMON! But after many hours of research, I'm not sure of anything...sometimes I think Reptilian, Demon, shapeshifter. I have read everything possible to come to a conclusion. This has haunted me for the last five years."

"About her touching me, well, she touched my face around my chin area...you know like when you touch a child's face and say 'Oh you're so cute!' That was kind of the theme. She had those sharp, pointy nails that all the young, trendy people are wearing these days, like Rihanna. Anyway, she touched my face more than once, and it made me feel very uncomfortable and she actually jabbed me a little. She just also had a very masculine way of moving.... She was not a big person but she moved kind of stiff when she danced, not fluid, not sexy."

Dinah reports that her chin where the woman touched her began to itch and burn, like an allergic reaction, in the aftermath of the encounter. She also broke out with a few hives. As her energy was being sucked away, Dinah watched the woman's face distort, and her mouth elongate on one side towards her ear. The woman's eyes glowed with an eerie reflection like an animal's, "luminous...! Like they were creating their own light."

Dinah has sought answers since the incident occurred, never understanding exactly what she confronted, and never able to shake the experience from her memory.

"I must tell you that this has been with me every day since and I can't put it down. I want to know why she took my energy, if she can follow me, if she can still hurt me. Do they have a mental connection once they have touched us?"

Dinah still feels the fear of the encounter, and is convinced that whatever the woman in the club really was, she did not have good intentions. "It was the horror and emptiness that she had, that touched me on the inside."

Metro Encounter

Andy had a similar, though much briefer experience while living in Washington D.C.:

"I was riding the Metro into the city. I rode it every day, and you see some questionable people but I usually just tried to ignore them. The ride wasn't that long for me. One day, I got on the Metro and the next stop, this guy gets on. He walked around the car as we were moving to the next stop, he seemed kind of nervous. There weren't a lot of people, but I was standing, holding on to one of the poles. This guy walked up to me and said, "I think you dropped your paper." I didn't have a paper, and the odd thing was he didn't have one either, and there wasn't a paper on the floor or anything. I shook my head and said no. He reached out and put his hand on my arm. When he did, I had a sharp pain in my solar plexus. I snatched my hand away.

Just then, the train stopped and I jumped off, even though it wasn't my stop. I turned and looked back as the doors were closing and that guy was standing there smirking at me. I was suddenly very tired. I had to sit down on a bench for awhile, and I kept feeling like I wanted to fall asleep. Finally, I got up and went and caught a cab home. I was tired all evening and slept in late the next day. By lunch that day, I felt fine, but I tell you that guy somehow sucked some of my energy from me."

By their accounts, both Andy and Dinah ran into something that was physical in nature but drained them of energy. While such an idea may sound far-fetched, we must bear in mind that native cultures around the world have long spoken of the human energy field, and in recent times science has finally admitted the human body does indeed have an 'aura' or energy field around it. What if something out there has a way to tap into that field, and deprive us of our natural energy and health? Whether at night in the darkness of the bedroom, or in broad daylight on a busy subway, there may be energy thieves around us, waiting for an opportunity to strike.

Chapter Nine
The Tendrils of the Slenderman

The Slenderman

Imagine a tall figure in a black suit. His face, if there is one, lies hidden in the shadows, with just a glimpse of pale, unnatural skin. He has impossibly long arms reaching out like slim tendrils; grasping at those who get too close. Strangely, it seems there are more than just two arms, and octopus-like, they move constantly, making it difficult even to be sure of what you're seeing. This figure has been seen in schoolyards, outside of homes and at sites where disasters have occurred. He is a nightmare figure, haunting the dreams of many, and blamed for the disappearance of both children and adults through the ages. He is the Slenderman. However, is he real or a complete work of fiction?

By most accounts, it seems the Slenderman was born from something awful —that is, the 'Something Awful' website and its forums. In 2009 members of the forum were called to participate in a contest. The challenge was to create a fake photograph that depicted something paranormal in nature. There was more however. Once the fake photo was created, it had to be promoted on the Internet as the genuine article. Those with an interest in the paranormal had to be convinced the subject of the photoshopped image was real.

The results seem to be far beyond what the originators imagined. In a brief time, the Slenderman meme rapidly traveled to all corners of the web. A video series was posted, an ARG (Alternate Reality Game) was created and countless blogs appeared to discuss this weird being. Tales were passed via Twitter, Facebook, email and discussion boards. The Slenderman, it seemed, was gaining momentum.

The Myth Unfolds

The modern Slenderman mythos began in May of 2009. On May first, a member on the Something Awful forums by the name of "Gerogerigegege" opened a new thread and issued this challenge:

"Creating paranormal images has been a hobby of mine for quite some time. Occasionally, I stumble upon odd websites showcasing strange photos, and I always wondered if it were possible to get one of my own chops in a book, documentary, or website just by casually leaking it out into the Web -whether they'd be supplements to bogus stories or not."

Once the contest was opened, a barrage of photoshopped pictures and creepy stories followed. Haunted objects and weird creatures were in abundance but nothing lit the community on fire like the images posted on June 10th.

Answering the paranormal-oriented challenge was forum member 'Victor Surge'. Surge's photos were fairly simplistic and that seemed to be part of their power. By choosing a subtle route, Surge created a mystery open to interpretation but contained a disturbing, underlying tone. The initial photos and their brief descriptions placed the "Slender Man" in the mid-1980s. The scant information included allowed those reading to leap to numerous conclusions and imaginations ran wild. One photo is credited as 'photographer unknown, presumed dead.' It shows a group of people who appear to be running from a strange, tall figure lurking in the background.

The second photo is more disturbing. It depicts a playground scene with several schoolchildren on and around a play set. In the background near a tree is a figure, barely discernible in the shadows, with several children around him. A brief statement accompanied this picture:

"One of two recovered photographs from the Stirling City Library blaze. Notable for being taken the day which fourteen children vanished and for what is referred to as "The Slender Man." Deformities cited as film defects by officials. Fire at library occurred one week later. Actual photograph confiscated as evidence. 1986, photographer: Mary Thomas, missing since June 13th, 1986."

This description appears to be the first use of the name "Slender Man" to define the mysterious being. The name quickly morphed into the now common "Slenderman."

The next day, June 11th, Surge added a document, which he claimed was a police report from 1955. The report was covered with scribbled notes and what were purported to be bloodstains. Among the notes was the statement: "Slenderman, Slenderman, kill us already, kill us, kill, kill, kill."

Victor Surge continued to add material to the thread. Drawings done by children, clippings from newspapers, more photographs with a thin, barely discernible figure hiding behind trees, and statements from those who had encountered the Slenderman. At this point there was still little known about the dreaded being. It was implied he was responsible for disappearances, loss of life and perhaps disasters. It was clear he was something otherworldly and that he invoked terror in those he stalked.

As the postings continued, adjustments were made to the myth. Users seemed to appreciate the more subtle aspects of the myth since it left more to the imagination. Member "WoodrowSkillson" posted: "...its better when you don't notice them (the tentacles) at first, and only later you realize just how alien the Slender Man is."

Victor Surge was very active on the forum and when asked about the Slenderman's origins responded:

"The Slender Man as an idea was made-up off the top of my head, although the concept is based on a number of things that scare me. The name I thought up on the fly when I wrote that first bit." Surge also stated on the forum:

"Having an unearthly creature, such as a skinwalker or something stalking you has always been much scarier than ghosts in my opinion." The Slenderman quickly moved beyond its initial inception by Victor Surge. Others began to add to the mythos and the figure blended with various bogeymen of the past, growing and morphing into an even more disturbing creation.

A poster named "Thoreau-Up" advanced the mythos by tying the Slenderman into the past, claiming the creature's origins went back to German medieval folk tales. He writes:

"I've been following the signs for quite some time. There are woodcuts dated back to the 16th century in Germany featuring a tall, disfigured man with only white spheres where his eyes should be.

They called him "Der Grofsmann," the tall man. He was a fairy who lived in the Black Forest. Bad children who crept into the woods at night would be chased by the slender man, and he wouldn't leave them alone until he caught them, or the child told the parents what he or she had done."

Thoreau-Up goes a few steps further by posting an account from "an old journal, dating around 1702" and "translated from German." The entry tells the tale of a child's abduction:

"My child, my Lars...He is gone. Taken from his bed. The only thing that we found was a scrap of black clothing. It feels like cotton, but it is softer... thicker. Lars came into my bedroom yesterday, screaming at the top of his lungs that "the angel is outside!", I asked him what he was talking about, and he told me some nonsense fairy story about Der Grofsmann. He said he went into the groves by our village and found one of my cows dead, hanging from a tree. I thought nothing of it at first...but now, he is gone. We must find Lars, and my family must leave before we are killed. I am sorry my son... I should have listened. May God forgive me."

Within a week, the Slenderman's history expanded greatly. Aside from countless modern tales, there were now stories that placed him in the Middle Ages, and even further back to Lower Egypt, circa 3100 BC. It seemed there was no stopping the development of this legend and it was about to take another leap forward.

The Buzz of Marble Hornets

The next significant phase in the development of the Slenderman came in the form of video. The first of many was a series called "Marble Hornets." The unfolding tale of Marble Hornets is narrated by "Jay," a friend of the film's producer. Marble Hornets was purported to be a student film that detailed the story of a twenty-something's return to his childhood home. The project took place over two months with periodic scenes being shot and directed by Alex, the man behind the film. Most of the film took place outside, close to the director's home in a wooded area, in an attempt to replicate a rural small town. After two months, Alex suddenly ended the project without explanation. His only comment was that he found "unworkable conditions" at the shooting location. Jay found the situation odd. Soon after he received the news from Alex, he noticed the director became distant and began to avoid everyone, choosing to sit alone in his house. Jay finally visited Alex at his home. According to his tale on the Marble Hornets website, he was quite disturbed when he saw Alex:

"Something about him was worse than I'd originally thought. He had lost a good bit of weight, and looked pretty sickly. I pretended like I didn't notice and we just hung out for awhile. Right before I left, I asked him about Marble Hornets and what he was planning on doing with all of his tapes of raw footage. With almost no hesitation, he simply said, "burn them." This caught me off guard. When I asked why he didn't just archive them for B-roll in future projects, he just said he never wanted to work with the footage again. He was completely serious about this. I couldn't understand why he'd just want to get rid of it completely. Surely, it wasn't all that useless. So I asked if I could take a look at them."

According to the story, Alex allowed Jay to look at the tapes under the condition that they never be returned and that Jay never discuss what was on the tapes. He also tried to discourage Jay from showing the tapes to anyone else. Alex showed Jay to the attic where the tapes were stored:

"There were tons of them. He grabbed a couple of plastic shopping bags and piled the tapes in and gave them to me, then shooed me out of the attic. Right as I was walking out the door, he said in the most serious tone I've ever heard from someone, "I'm not kidding, don't ever bring this up around me again.""

Alex's comment was so sudden that I didn't have time to react before he had closed the door on me. He transferred to an out-of-state school soon after that and I haven't seen him since."

Jay claimed he put the whole incident out of his mind and the tapes remained unwatched for a period of time. Eventually, he began going through the footage and posting clips from the tapes.

Marble Hornets is essentially a part of the genre of 'found footage' made popular by films such as *The Blair Witch Project* and *Paranormal Activity*. As the video clips are revealed, viewers learn that Alex was being stalked by a being he calls "The Operator," aka the Slenderman. Once Jay begins posting the video clips on the Internet, Alex disappears. Jay then begins to document his search for Alex and his attempts to uncover the mystery of the Operator/Slenderman.

As of early 2013, the Marble Hornets website is still active and posting continues. Because of the interactive nature of Marble Hornets, it's considered an ARG (alternate reality game). In this format, people are free to post their responses and their own videos to contribute to the story. The lines between fact and fiction are blurred in this format by the addition of news items and current and past events tied into the overall story.

Marble Hornets reveals that the presence of the Slenderman has an effect on audio and visual recording equipment. Strange noises and interference show up on tracks recorded when he is near. Visual images are distorted and sometimes only static or strange shapes are captured. In the course of the series, we also learn he has an affinity with doorways and that he may control where they lead. He emerges from rooms shown to be empty and he lures people to doorways that lead to strange locations other than the rooms that should be there.

We also learn other things about the Slenderman throughout the series. His effect on the people who encounter him is far-reaching. They experience physical pains, coughing fits and other strange episodes. They black out and lose time, performing actions they later have no recall of. Slowly, they slip into the depths of madness. The material added in the Marble Hornets video represent another defining piece of the Slenderman mythos and set the course for the continued growth of the tales.

Of Nightmares and Tulpas

On November 6th, 2009, the popular radio talk show Coast to Coast AM with George Noory received a series of phone calls from people expressing their concern about a creature that terrified them. Some of the callers reported seeing a tall, thin entity without a face. It was the Slenderman. Most disturbing, while some callers claimed this being was plaguing their nightmares, others claimed they had seen him in the physical, waking world.

It would be easy to dismiss such accounts and believe the callers were mistaken, delusional or even fabricating the stories, but this was not the first time people have professed that the nightmare creature was a flesh and blood being. If we are to believe these accounts, it seems as though the Slenderman has leapt from the virtual pages of Internet blogs and stepped into the real world. Is such a thing possible? According to some ancient traditions, yes it is.

Consider this chilling statement, issued early in the Slenderman discussion on the Something Awful forum. It was posted by a user simply known as "I." It read: "The Slender Man. He exists because you thought of him. Now try and not think of him." The statement's implication brings to mind the Tibetan concept of the Tulpa. There's no exact translation into English for this term but the most common understanding is "Thoughtform."

The Tulpa legend is connected to Tibetan Buddhism and mystic traditions. In simplest terms, the creation of a Tulpa, according to eastern teachings, is a process to bring a thought into physical existence. Through willpower, the strength of the mind and focus, the Tulpa is created. Tibetan teachers believe by following a specific set of meditations and rituals, a concentrated thought can become physical. This mental projection moves from the mind's eye to the physical world. First in the form of a shadowy, ghost-like figure; eventually, as mental energy continues to be fed into the Tulpa, it takes on full, physical life. Once created the Tulpa can eventually detach from its creator and proceed to live its own life, unconstrained by the originator's initial thoughts. At this point, the Tulpa seeks energy from other sources to continue its existence.

On the surface, it does not appear this process was carried out during the creation of the Slenderman. Certainly there's no indication anyone performed a process to specifically create this being. However, there are other possibilities to consider in terms of the Tulpa/Slenderman connection.

Is it possible that if enough people believe in something that this belief alone can give it life? What are the consequences of a mass number of minds focused on a singular concept such as the Slenderman?

Despite the fact the Slenderman can be traced back to his Internet origins and his fabrication during a forum challenge, the legend spread at an amazing pace and he quickly became an Internet meme. Slenderman spread like a virus and everyone involved had some influence, adding energy to the creation. The concept itself is driven by fear and paranoia; powerful, base emotions that generate high levels of energy. The human mind, hearing Slenderman stories, often runs away with itself. It's easy to imagine tall figures lurking in the trees, just out of sight. The psychic energy of so many people focused on such emotions might well produce, even briefly, a physical manifestation. Such a creation could also play into suppressed memories or emotional traumas of the past. The human mind doesn't like blank spots, and will attempt to "fill in the blanks" even with something strange or unsettling. I've received countless communications from people who firmly believe they have encountered the Slenderman at some point in their lives. Many of the stories predate the Internet creation point by years.

"I remember seeing a figure like this when I was a child in Ohio" writes Matt. "I know that I saw it. I remember having horrible dreams for the longest time but my parents kept telling me I was just having nightmares and there wasn't really anything out there. But he was; I know that he was out there every night for a whole summer. He was always standing in the trees at the back of the yard, and from my bed I could see him. I don't know what finally made him go away, but I know that I prayed every night that he wouldn't harm me when I fell asleep."

Taken by itself, Matt's childhood recall could be dismissed as dreams or incomplete memories of a difficult period in his life. Matt's story doesn't end there, however, because he saw the same figure as an adult.

"I was almost thirty years old and I had a strange experience. I was living in Indiana and working for a computer firm. It was a pretty good job, not too much stress and the money was decent. I was at work late one night because we were having a send-off party for a co-worker. There was no alcohol involved so I wasn't intoxicated. I got home and went straight up stairs to go to bed. I didn't even turn the light on in my bedroom, just got my suit and shoes off and went to lay down. Just before I got in bed, I noticed something odd outside in the back yard. I walked over to the window and there it was, that same weird figure I had seen in my childhood —standing by a couple of trees, waving its long arms about. I felt very, very afraid in that moment. All my childhood fears had returned. I jumped into bed and did something I had not done in years. I prayed that I would be safe and that it would just leave me alone."

Some versions of the Slenderman legend say that once you see him as a child, he will follow you until you die, always there in the background, waiting. In conveying his story to me, Matt never called the being Slenderman. In fact he told me he was never sure what to call it, simply that it was a disturbing being and he wanted no part of it. Matt gave me his account in 2004, well before the Slenderman mythos began in 2009.   His is not the only such story I have received. Take this account for instance. It came from a woman named Janet who recounts some of her experiences with a figure that has lurked in the shadows of her life since childhood.

"I grew up in a rural area of Virginia. We lived in an old house and it had a lot of trees around it. There was a little clear space in the back yard, but it went right up to some thick woods that were behind the house. My sisters and I mostly played in the front yard because it was bigger and had more grassy areas. When I was about ten, I started waking up at night. It happened night after night. I would wake up at about two in the morning. Usually I would just lay there and try to get back to sleep, not wanting to get in trouble for being up so late. One night when I was laying there, I heard sounds outside. Since it was summer, my bedroom window was open and it had a screen in it to let the air in. My room was on the second floor and it looked out over the back yard. The sound was a scratching noise and I thought maybe one of our cats had got stuck outside. I went and looked out of my window to try to see what the sound was coming from. I looked down and to the right. I could see the back door from my window because it jutted out a bit. The moon was bright enough to give some light, but I couldn't see any cat there.

I stood there looking around the yard. The scratching noise had stopped and the wind had picked up a little bit. Then I noticed something moving at the back of the yard, right where the woods started. It was too dark to really tell what it was, but it seemed to be something very tall by the trees. I watched it move and knew it wasn't a tree because it was walking along the line of the woods. Then it just stopped and I had the most awful feeling that whatever it was, it was staring at me. I felt really, really afraid and I ran to my bed, ducking under the covers and staying there until morning. By the next day, I had convinced myself that it had all been a bad dream. I continued to wake up at night for a while, but I didn't get up again to look out of the window, just in case. A couple of years passed and the next incident that I clearly remember happened when I was almost thirteen.

We were still living in the same house and I was still in the same bedroom. I hadn't really thought about the earlier incident, I guess at that age there were plenty of things to occupy my mind. Suddenly though, I started having trouble sleeping. Like before, I started waking up late in the night between one and three am. I would lay there and try to fall back asleep, which sometimes took awhile. It was on one of those nights I was laying there when I heard what sounded like a laugh. It was distant and I could tell it was coming from outside in the yard. The sound was drifting up through my window. I got out of bed right away to see where it was coming from. Standing there looking out of the window, I remembered what I had seen when I was ten. It all came back to me in a rush at the same time I noticed movement at the back of the yard, by the tree line. The fear came back too.

This has continued throughout my life. Every few years I fall back into the pattern of not being able to sleep in the middle of the night, always between the times of one and three am. I start waking up and have trouble getting back to sleep for a few hours. No matter where I've lived, even in different states, the pattern starts and I start waking up and I catch glimpses of this thing, whatever it is, outside of my window. For awhile, I lived in a large city in an apartment building. When I started waking up while living there, I thought, no way will that thing be here in the city— but it was. Still there, lurking outside of my bedroom, always watching.

Over the years, I've seen glimpses of him, or it. It's a very, very tall man and his arms are impossibly long. I've never seen a face, just glimpses of his head, which I can tell is bald. I've always felt as if it's just waiting for me to come outside, to see it closer and find out what it is. I think that's what it wants, but I don't think I would ever come back if I went out there.

I relish the times when I'm able to sleep the whole night through, and not have to think about it lurking outside. Sadly though, I've come to believe I'll never be free of this thing until I pass away. I don't think it can ever harm me though, as long as I stay in the safety of my home and don't answer its call on those dark nights."

Janet is not alone in having recurring visits from a shadowy figure. Randall contacted me about his sightings of a strange man he saw on several occasions growing up.

"I started seeing him when I was in my early teens. I think I was about fourteen the first time he appeared, at least that's the first time I remember seeing him. At first he was outside around the trees in the yard. I first noticed him one evening when my brother and I were outside tossing a football back and forth. My brother missed a catch because I threw it high. The ball landed near the tress behind him and I stood there and watched as he went to get it. He picked the ball up and turned back towards me, that's when I saw a weird figure in the trees behind him. It must have been seven feet tall and it had very long arms. I just stared at it because I couldn't believe what I was seeing. I couldn't take my eyes off it. It was moving very slowly sideways, and I could see the long arms kind of swinging around. My brother threw the football and it just went past me, I guess. He was calling to me but I didn't hear him, it was as though I was entranced. He finally came over and gave me a shove on the shoulder telling me to snap out of it. I guess jarring me was enough because I looked at him, asked him if he had seen 'it' and pointed to the trees. He turned and looked at the trees saying 'what? There's nothing there'. After that, we went inside but I couldn't shake the feeling that there was something out there watching me, or maybe us. For the next few days, I kept catching glimpses of it around the outside of the house. My brother kept asking what was wrong with me because I didn't want to be outside anymore.

At some point, the thing just went away or I stopped seeing it, I'm not sure which. Either way, I forgot about it for a time. The next year my brother and I went to a summer camp. The first few days there were great, we made lots of friends and there was plenty to do. Then one evening, just as it was getting dark I saw it again. It was lurking in the trees and it was closer this time, so I got a better look at it. The figure looked like a man at least seven or eight feet tall. His arms were long, they seemed too long, it wasn't natural how far out he could reach with them. He was wearing a black suit and his face was very pale. I couldn't see any of his features enough to describe him. I ran back to the cabin as quick as I could, I just wanted to get away from him.

It got really creepy the next day though, because another kid saw him. We had met a boy from Germany. His family had just moved to the United States early that year. He spoke English but he had an accent and when he got excited, he would start speaking in German. The day after I had seen the creepy figure in the woods, this boy came running into the cabin that we all shared. He was yelling in German and pointing outside. A couple of the other guys went outside to see what he was talking about but they came in saying there was nothing there. I felt a chill run up my spine though, because I knew what he was talking about. When he calmed down, he wouldn't tell anyone what he had seen. They kept asking but they were also teasing him, saying he must have gotten scared of a raccoon or something. Later that evening I went up to him and took a chance. I told him what I had seen the night before. His eyes grew big when I told my story and he kept shaking his head. 'It is Der Schwarze Mann!' I later learned from

171

him, after he calmed down, he told me more about this legend from old Germany. It was supposed to be a menacing, shadowy man who lurked around waiting to steal children."

Other investigators of strange phenomena have received accounts of Slenderman and associated beings. Pastor Robin Swope is the author of the excellent book, *"Slenderman: From Fiction to Fact."* Swope chronicles the rise of Slenderman from its inception on the Internet through its development and growth. He also includes numerous related accounts he has collected in his years of paranormal research. Swope breaks this section of his book down into three parts: General Encounters, Specific Encounters and Alien Encounters. General Encounters involve accounts describing entities that loosely fit the Slenderman mythos. The section on Specific Encounters details accounts that fit perfectly into typical Slenderman tales. The final portion involves Alien Encounters and their similarities to the Slenderman. As Pastor Swope says in his book:

"After reading of Slenderman, I realized that even before the being was "created" on the Internet, people from all walks of life had been encountering this creature in one way or the other. And since the Meme became famous, these encounters have multiplied exponentially."

Like myself and other investigators, Pastor Swope has files of accounts he received well before the Internet creation that bear a striking resemblance to the Slenderman.

"...one is left with two simple options. The witnesses are either lying or telling the truth," says Swope. Indeed, much of the study of the paranormal comes down to the facts presented by the witnesses and their recall of events. People who outright lie about their paranormal encounters are not as prevalent as skeptics would like us to believe. When looking at reports of such phenomena, there is a portion of cases that can be explained by mistaken identity. Pareidolia is also a consideration. This is a psychological phenomenon that involves perceiving something significant within images or sounds. An example of this is seeing the shapes of clouds as animals or other objects.

Swope had a brush with "something" himself when he began to delve into the phenomenon. Although he does not claim it was the Slenderman, he does question the power of such concentrated, negative energy. In his book he examines the Slenderman from many angles, but leaves the possibilities open as to exactly what the phenomenon is, calling us to question both the reality and the fiction of this weird creature.

Despite a brief history, the Slenderman has found his way into many corners of the mainstream. He appeared in a music video for the song "Equinox" by Skrillex. He is the focus of a video game called Slender and appears to be the inspiration for the "Enderman" in the game Minecraft. Slenderman's influence can also be seen in movies and television, either as himself or in a thinly-veiled guise. He may have been an inspiration, at least on some level, for a 2012 movie titled "The Tall Man" that deals with the disappearance of children in a small town.

On the other hand, Slenderman's image was likely influenced by entertainment such as the popular television series *Buffy the Vampire Slayer*. One of the series' most remembered episodes featured demons known as "the gentlemen," garbed in dark suits and having pale skin and bald heads. They moved in an eerie fashion and created silence around them as they carried out their dark deeds.

The Slenderman holds a unique place in paranormal lore. Clear fictional roots are obvious, yet countless people now believe this being is a genuine phenomenon. Co-created it seems, via a combination of elements made possible in modern times with the advent of the Internet, a gateway to new levels of mass consciousness. We have to consider these possibilities carefully as communication and connection continues to evolve.

The Slender Future

Moving forward, it seems the Slenderman will continue to play a role in the world of the paranormal and pop culture. *Variety* magazine recently reported that the rights for a big screen adaptation of the Marble Hornets series had been opted by Mosaic Media Group. A Slenderman movie would certainly solidify this disturbing figure in the minds of the masses. Parsec Productions, the makers of the successful viral Internet game, "Slender: The Eight Pages" is launching a sequel titled "Slender: The Arrival" due out in late 2013.

Perhaps the Slenderman is merely a modern myth still in the making, a boogeyman for the 2000s that will scare children and give adults a slight pause when unexplained noises are heard from dark corners. If so, then he will continue to show up on both the small and big screens of entertainment, and over time he will evoke nervous laughter and chills on movie night.

There is a darker possibility, though. It may be that the collective consciousness of numerous people, spread far and wide, have co-created something quite disturbing. A modern tulpa feeding off the fear and dread created in the stories and legends being written about him. If this is the case, then there is indeed cause for concern for the only boundaries to his power lie in the minds of those giving him life.

Bibliography

Al-Ashqar, Umar S. *The World of Jinn and Devils*. Somerset, NJ: IIPH Publishing, 2005.

Allen, W.K. *Crocodile-Skinned Entities at Calgary, Flying Saucer Review*, 1974

Balzano, Christopher. *Dark Woods*. Atglen, PA: Schiffer Books, 2007.

Balzano, Christopher. *Ghost of the Bridgewater Triangle*. Atglen, PA: Schiffer Books, 2008

Barber, Paul. *Vampires, Burial and Death*. New Haven, CT: Yale University Press 1988.

Bondeson, Jan. *The London Monster: A Sanguinary Tale*. Cambridge, MA: Da Capo Press, 2000.

Brennan, J.H. *Occult Tibet: Secret Practices of Himalayan Magic*. Woodbury, MN: Llewellyn Worldwide Publishing, 20002.

Briggs, Katharine. *An Encyclopedia of Fairies, Hobgoblins, Brownies, Boogies and Other Supernatural Creatures*. New York, NY: Pantheon Books, 1976.

Broome, Fiona. Hollow Hill Website.

Burton, Richard Francis. *The Book of the Thousand Nights and One Night*. New York, NY: Assouline Press, 2006.

Cheung, Theresa. *The Element Encyclopedia of Vampires: An A-Z of the Undead*. New York, NY: Element Books/Harper, 2009.

Clark, Jerome. *The UFO Encyclopedia Vols 1 & 2. Second Edition*. Detroit, MI: Omnigraphics, Inc. 1998.

Clark, Jerome. *Unexplained! 347 Strange Sightings, Incredible Occurrences, and Puzzling Physical Phenomena.* Visible Ink Press, Detroit 1993

Coleman, Loren. *Mysterious America.* New York, NY: Gallery Books, 2007.

Curran, Bob Dr. *Vampires. Franklin Lakes,* NJ: Career Press, 2005.

Dalrymple, William. *City of Djinns: A Year in Delhi.* New York, NY: Harper Collins Publishing, 1994.

Dash, Mike. *Spring-Heeled Jack, Fortean Studies Vol 3. Bel Air,* CA: SOS Free Stock, 1996

Derenberger, Harold W. *Visitors From Lanulos.* Burlington, VT: Vantage Press, 1971

di Stefano, Rino. *Il Caso Zanfretta (The Zanfretta Case).* De Ferrari Press, 2012.

Fortune, Dion. *Psychic Self-Defense; The Classic Instruction Manual for Protecting Yourself Against Paranormal Attack,* 1930 edition. New York, NY: Weiser Books, revised edition, 2011.

Fritz, Jean. *The Good Giants and the Bad Pukwudgies.* New York, NY: Putnam Press, 1989.

Guiley, Rosemary Ellen. *Encyclopedia of Demons & Demonology.* New York, NY: Checkmark Books, 2009.

Guiley, Rosemary, Ellen. *The Djinn Connection.* New Milford, CT: Visionary Living Inc., 2013.

Guiley, Rosemary Ellen & Imbrogno, Philip J. *The Vengeful Djinn.* Woodbury, MN: Llewellyn Worldwide, 2011.

Haining, Peter. *The Legend and Bizarre Crimes of Spring Heeled Jack.* Frederick Muller Ltd: Uk edition, 1977.

Hanauer, J.E. *Folklore of the Holy Land: Moslem, Christian and Jewish (1901).* Ithaca, NY: Cornell University Press, 2009.

Hufford, David J. *The Terror That Comes In The Night: An experience- centered study of supernatural assault traditions.* Philadelphia, PA: University of Pennsylvania Press, 1982.

Keel, John A. *The Mothman Prophecies*. New York, NY: Saturday Review Press/E.P. Dutton and Company, 1975.

Keel, John A. *The Complete Guide To Mysterious Beings*. New York, NY: TOR Books, 1970.

Kramer, Heinrich & Sprenger, James. Summers, Montague (translator). *Malleus Male Carum (The Hammer of the Witches)*. Mineola, NY: Dover Publications, 1971.

Leeming, David. *Oxford Companion to World Mythology*. New York, NY: Oxford University Press, 2009.

Lebling, Robert. *Legends of the Fire Spirits: Jinn and Genies from Arabia to Zanziba*r. Berkley, CA: Counterpoint Press, 2001.

Lecouteux, Claude. *The Secret History of Vampires*. *Rochester*, VT: Inner Traditions Press, 1999.

Magor, John. *Our UFO Visitors*. Seattle, WA: Hancock House Publishers Inc., 1977.

Masello, Robert. *Fallen Angels and Spirits of the Dark*. New York, NY: Berkley Publishing Group, 1995.

Maruna, Scott. *Mad Gasser of Mattoon: Dispelling the Hysteria*. Jacksonville, IL: Swamp Gas Book Co. 2003

Matthews, John & Matthews, Caitlin. *The Element Encyclopedia of Magical Creatures: The Ultimate A-Z of Fantastic Beings from Myth and Magic*. New York, NY: Sterling Publishing, 2005.

Musgrave, Brent. *UFO Occupants & Critters*. New York, NY: Global Communications, 1979.

Newton, Michael. *Strange Indiana Monsters*. Atglen, PA: Schiffer Books, 2006.

Nye, Catrin. *Possession, Jinn and Britain's Backstreet Exorcists*. BBC News, November, 2012.

Proud, Louis. *Dark Intrusions*. San Antonio, TX: Anomalist Books, 2009.

Redfern, Nick. *Contactees*. Pompton Plains, NJ: New Page Books, 2009.

Robinson, Charles Turek. *The New England Ghost Files*. North Attleboro, MA: Covered Bridge Press, 1994

Rose, Carol. *Spirits, Fairies, Leprechauns and Goblins: An Encyclopedia*. New York, NY: W.W. Norton & Company, 1998.

Rutkowski, Chris A. *I Saw It Too!* Toronto, ON, Canada: Dundurn Press, 2009.

Shah, Indries. *Secret Lore of Magic*. Secaucus, NJ: Carol Pub Group, 1970.

Shuker, Karl. *Extraordinary Animals Revisited*. North Devon, UK: CFZ Press, 2007.

Simmons, William S. *Spirit of the New England Tribes*. Lebanon, NH: University Press of New England, 1986.

Steiger, Brad. *Real Aliens, Space Beings, and Creatures from Other Worlds*. Canton, MI: Visible Ink Press, 2011.

Steiger, Brad. *Real Vampires, Night Stalkers, and Creatures from the Darkside*. Canton, MI: Visible Ink Press, 2009.

Swope, Robin. *Slenderman: From Fiction To Fact*. Open Gate Press, 2012.

Taymeeyah, Ibn. *Ibn Taymeeyah's Essay on the Jinn*. New Delhi, India: Islamic Books Services, 2002, 2004)

Vincent, Ian 'Cat.' *The Slenderman; Tracing the birth and evolution of a modern monster, Darklore Volume Six*. Brisbane, Australia: Daily Grail Publishing, 2011.

Weatherly, David. *The Black Eyed Children*. Arizona: Leprechaun Press, 2012.

About the Author

David Weatherly is a renaissance man of the strange and supernatural. He has traveled the world in pursuit of ghosts, cryptids, UFOs, magic, and more. From the specters of dusty castles, to remote, haunted islands, from ancient sites, to modern mysteries, he has journeyed to the most unusual places on the globe seeking the unknown.

David became fascinated with the paranormal at a young age. Ghost stories and accounts of weird creatures and UFOs led him to discover many of his early influences. Writers such as John Keel, Jacques Vallee, Hans Holzer, and others set him on course to spend his life exploring and investigating the unexplained.

Throughout his life, he's also delved into shamanic and magical traditions from around the world, spending time with elders from numerous cultures in Europe, the Americas, Africa and Asia. He has studied with Taoist masters in China, Tibetan Lamas, and other mystics from the far east. He's picked up knowledge from African and Native American tribal elders and sat around fires with shamans from countless other traditions.

Along his path, David has also gathered a lot of arcane knowledge, studying a range of ancient arts from palmistry, the runes, and other obscure forms of divination, to alchemy and magick. He has studied and taught Qigong and Ninjutsu, as well as various energy related arts. David has also studied stage and performance magic.

His shamanic and magical background has given him a unique perspective in his explorations into the unknown, and he continues to write, travel and explore, leaving no stone unturned in his quest for the strange and unusual.

David has investigated, and written about, a diverse range of topics including, Hauntings & Ghosts, Cryptozoology, Ufology, Ancient Mysteries, Shamanism, Magic and Psychic Phenomena.

David is the founder of the independent media and publishing company, Eerie Lights Publishing.

He has been a featured speaker at conferences around the world and has lectured for countless paranormal and spiritual groups.

He is a frequent guest on Coast to Coast AM with George Noory, Spaced Out Radio and other radio programs. David has also appeared on numerous television shows including the Travel Channel's Mysteries of the Outdoors, History Channel's Ancient Aliens, Beyond Belief and other programs. He was also featured in the highly successful series On the Trail of UFOs.

David's books include Strange Intruders, Eerie Companions, the Haunted series, the Wood Knocks series, and the Monsters of America series.

Find David online at:

https://eerielights.com/

Made in the USA
Coppell, TX
04 October 2022

84076182R00116